Advanced Bank Statement Mortgage Loan Structuring

How to Engineer Approvals Using Deposits, Expense Ratios, and Investor Guidelines

By Joseph G. Correa

Licensed Mortgage Broker

Finibi Mortgage

Copyright & Legal Notice

Published by Live Stronger Faster

The information provided in this book is for educational and informational purposes only and does not constitute financial, legal, tax, or investment advice. Although the author is a licensed mortgage professional, the content presented is general in nature and is not intended as personalized guidance for any specific individual or financial situation.

The strategies, structuring methods, and examples discussed in this book are illustrative and educational in nature. They are intended to demonstrate concepts related to bank statement mortgage loan qualification and structuring, including deposit analysis, expense ratio application, and investor guideline interpretation. These examples do not represent guaranteed outcomes or approvals. Results may vary significantly based on individual financial profiles, documentation, credit history, property type, and lender-specific requirements.

The author and publisher make no representations or warranties regarding the accuracy, completeness, or applicability of the content and disclaim any liability for errors, omissions, or outcomes resulting from the use or misuse of the information contained in this book.

All trademarks, service marks, company names, and product names referenced in this publication are the property of their respective owners and are used strictly for identification and educational purposes only. Their inclusion does not imply endorsement or affiliation.

First Edition, 2026

Table of Contents

Introduction

This is where strategy replaces guesswork, where average files become strong approvals, and where denied loans are transformed into closed transactions through precision, creativity, and deep understanding of lender behavior. If the earlier books taught you the rules, this book teaches you how to work within—and around—those rules to produce consistent, high-level results.

By now, you understand what bank statement loans are, how income is calculated, and how different borrower profiles are evaluated. You have learned how to read deposits, apply expense ratios, and identify red flags. But in the real world, deals are rarely perfect. Borrowers have inconsistencies. Income fluctuates. Credit may not be ideal. Documentation is often incomplete or misunderstood. This is where most loan files fail—and where top-level professionals separate themselves from the rest. Advanced structuring is the art of taking an imperfect file and presenting it in a way that aligns with investor guidelines while maximizing approval potential.

At its core, advanced bank statement mortgage structuring is about controlling three key variables: income presentation, risk perception, and lender alignment. Income presentation involves more than simply averaging deposits. It requires understanding how to isolate qualifying income, remove non-recurring deposits, and justify patterns that might otherwise raise concerns. Risk perception is how the underwriter views the borrower's overall profile, including credit history, reserves, property type, and loan purpose. Lender alignment is about matching the file to the right investor, program, and guideline set to ensure the highest likelihood of approval.

One of the most important concepts you will master in this book is the ability to engineer income through deposit analysis. Not all deposits are created equal. Some are recurring and stable, while others are one-time events that must be excluded. Some accounts reflect gross revenue, while others show net usable income. Advanced structuring involves identifying which accounts to use, which to exclude, and how to present the data in a clean, logical, and defensible format. It also involves knowing when to use personal bank statements, business bank statements, or a combination of both to achieve the best outcome.

Expense ratios play a critical role in this process. Many lenders apply a standard expense factor—often ranging from 10% to 50%—to business bank statement deposits. However, experienced professionals know that these ratios are not always fixed. They can be adjusted, supported, or replaced with alternative documentation such as a CPA-prepared profit and loss statement. Understanding when and how to influence the expense ratio can dramatically increase qualifying income and turn a marginal file into an approved loan.

Another advanced strategy involves layering compensating factors to offset weaknesses in a file. A borrower with lower credit may still qualify if they have strong reserves, a large down payment, or a stable income history. A borrower with fluctuating deposits may still be approved if the overall trend is positive and well-documented. The key is to build a complete story that explains the borrower's financial situation in a way that makes sense to the underwriter. This is not about hiding weaknesses—it is about addressing them proactively and presenting a balanced, well-supported file.

Investor guidelines vary widely across lenders, and understanding these differences is one of the most powerful tools you can develop. Some lenders are more flexible with credit scores. Others are more aggressive with loan-to-value ratios. Some allow higher expense factors, while others require stricter documentation. Advanced structuring means knowing where to send the loan before you even submit it. It means anticipating how each lender will interpret the file and positioning the loan accordingly. You will also learn how to structure loans based on specific borrower goals. Some borrowers want to maximize loan amount. Others want to minimize documentation. Some are focused on cash flow, while others are focused on long-term portfolio growth. Each of these goals requires a different approach. By understanding how to adjust income calculations, expense assumptions, and loan terms, you can create customized solutions that align with the borrower's objectives while still meeting lender requirements.

Another critical component of advanced structuring is managing documentation. Clean, organized, and consistent documentation can make the difference between a smooth approval and a delayed or denied loan. This includes properly labeling bank statements, explaining large deposits, documenting business activity, and ensuring that all supporting documents align with the income being presented. The goal is to eliminate confusion and reduce the number of questions the underwriter needs to ask.

Timing also plays a significant role in structuring bank statement loans. The difference between using 12 months versus 24 months of statements can impact income calculations significantly. In some cases, waiting a few months to allow stronger deposits to replace weaker ones can improve the borrower's profile. Understanding when to move forward and when to wait is a strategic decision that can greatly affect the outcome of the loan. In this book, you will explore real-world scenarios that demonstrate how advanced structuring works in practice. You will see how small adjustments in income calculation, expense ratios, or lender selection can lead to dramatically different results. You will learn how to identify opportunities within a file that others might overlook and how to turn those opportunities into approvals.

You will also gain insight into how underwriters think. Understanding the underwriting mindset is essential for advanced structuring. Underwriters are not looking for perfection—they are looking for consistency, logic, and documentation. When you can present a file that tells a clear and credible story, you make the underwriter's job easier, and approvals become more likely.

As you move through this book, you will begin to see bank statement loans not just as a product, but as a flexible framework that can be adapted to fit a wide range of borrower situations. This flexibility is what makes bank statement loans so powerful, but it also requires a higher level of skill and attention to detail. With that skill comes the ability to close more deals, serve more clients, and create more opportunities for both yourself and your borrowers.

The strategies you will learn here are designed to give you a competitive edge. Whether you are a loan officer, mortgage broker, real estate investor, or borrower, mastering advanced structuring will allow you to approach each deal with confidence and clarity. You will no longer rely on trial and error. Instead, you will have a structured process for analyzing, positioning, and closing bank statement loans at a high level.

This is the culmination of everything in the series. From understanding the fundamentals to working with complex borrower profiles, you are now stepping into the role of a strategist—someone who can see beyond the surface of a file and identify the best path forward. This is where deals get done, where clients get approved, and where true expertise is developed.

As you begin this final book, approach it with the mindset of mastery. Take the time to understand each concept, apply it to real scenarios, and refine your approach with each deal you encounter. The more you practice these strategies, the more natural they will become, and the more successful you will be in navigating the world of bank statement mortgage lending.

This is not just about closing loans. It is about building a system, a skill set, and a level of expertise that can create long-term success in the mortgage industry. The ability to structure complex deals is one of the most valuable skills you can develop, and it will continue to serve you as the market evolves and new opportunities emerge.

Welcome to advanced bank statement mortgage loan structuring—the highest level of this discipline.

Chapter 1

The Foundation of Advanced Bank Statement Mortgage Loan Structuring

Advanced bank statement mortgage loan structuring begins with a mindset shift. At the entry level, most professionals focus on whether a borrower qualifies. At the advanced level, the question changes to how a borrower can be positioned to qualify. This distinction is critical. Instead of reacting to guidelines, you begin to proactively shape the loan file to align with them. Every deposit, every document, and every financial detail becomes a tool that can be used strategically. The goal is no longer to simply submit a loan—it is to engineer an approval.

To understand advanced structuring, you must first recognize that bank statement loans are inherently flexible. Unlike traditional mortgage loans that rely heavily on tax returns and standardized income calculations, bank statement loans allow for interpretation. This flexibility creates opportunity, but it also requires precision. The same borrower can qualify for dramatically different loan amounts depending on how their income is calculated, which accounts are used, and how their financial story is presented. Advanced structuring is about controlling these variables to produce the strongest possible outcome. The first layer of this foundation is income identification. Not all deposits should be treated equally, and one of the biggest mistakes inexperienced professionals make is assuming that total deposits equal usable income. In reality, deposits must be analyzed, categorized, and filtered. Recurring deposits tied to business activity are the primary focus, while non-recurring deposits such as transfers, refunds, or one-time payments should typically be excluded. The ability to distinguish between these types of deposits is essential for building a credible income calculation.

Once income is identified, the next step is income stabilization. Lenders are not just looking at how much a borrower earns—they are looking at how consistent that income is over time. Fluctuations are common for self-employed borrowers, but patterns matter. An upward trend can be used as a strength, while erratic or declining income must be explained or mitigated. Advanced structuring involves selecting the appropriate time frame—whether 12 months or 24 months—and, in some cases, strategically timing the application to reflect stronger financial periods.

Expense ratio application is another critical component. Most lenders apply a standard expense factor to business bank statement deposits, but this is not always the optimal approach. Advanced professionals understand that expense ratios can be influenced through documentation and positioning. For example, a borrower with low operating expenses may benefit from a CPA-prepared profit and loss statement that justifies a lower expense ratio. By reducing the assumed expenses, the borrower's qualifying income increases, often significantly.

Another key principle is account selection. Borrowers may have multiple bank accounts—personal, business, or a mix of both. Each account tells a different story. Business accounts often reflect gross revenue, while personal accounts may show net income after expenses. Choosing the right combination of accounts can dramatically impact the outcome of the loan. In some cases, using only personal accounts provides a cleaner and more conservative income profile. In other cases, combining accounts allows for a more comprehensive view of the borrower's financial activity.

Risk layering is where structuring becomes more advanced. Every loan file contains strengths and weaknesses. The goal is to balance these elements in a way that makes the overall file acceptable to the lender. A borrower with a lower credit score may still qualify if they have strong income and significant reserves. A borrower with limited reserves may still be approved if they have excellent credit and stable income. Advanced structuring involves identifying these compensating factors and presenting them effectively. Loan-to-value ratio, or LTV, plays a major role in this process. A lower LTV reduces risk for the lender and can offset other weaknesses in the file. Borrowers who are close to qualifying may benefit from increasing their down payment or reducing the loan amount to achieve a more favorable LTV. Understanding how LTV interacts with other factors such as credit score and reserves allows you to make strategic adjustments that improve approval odds.

Reserves are another powerful tool in advanced structuring. Many borrowers underestimate the importance of having liquid assets after closing. However, strong reserves can significantly strengthen a file, especially for investment properties or higher-risk borrowers. Demonstrating that a borrower has the ability to cover several months of mortgage payments provides reassurance to the lender and can be the deciding factor in an approval.

Documentation is where strategy meets execution. Even the best-structured file can fail if the documentation is unclear, inconsistent, or incomplete. Advanced structuring requires meticulous attention to detail. Bank statements must be complete and legible. Large deposits must be explained. Business activity must align with the borrower's stated profession. Every document should support the narrative being presented. The goal is to create a file that is easy for the underwriter to understand and approve. Another important aspect of advanced structuring is lender selection. Not all lenders interpret guidelines the same way. Some are more conservative, while others are more flexible. Some specialize in certain borrower profiles, while others have broader programs. Matching the loan to the right lender is often just as important as structuring the file itself. This requires knowledge of multiple investors and their specific guidelines, as well as experience in understanding how they approach different types of files.

Communication also plays a critical role. Advanced professionals do not simply submit a loan and wait for a decision. They proactively communicate with underwriters, provide clear explanations, and address potential concerns before they become issues. This includes writing detailed loan summaries, organizing documentation logically, and anticipating questions that may arise during the underwriting process.

Timing and sequencing are often overlooked but can have a significant impact on the outcome of a loan. For example, paying down debt before applying can improve debt-to-income ratios. Waiting for stronger bank statement months can increase qualifying income. Even the order in which documents are presented can influence how the file is perceived. Advanced structuring involves thinking ahead and making decisions that position the borrower for success. As you build your foundation in advanced structuring, it is important to develop a systematic approach. Each file should be analyzed using a consistent framework: identify income, stabilize it, apply the appropriate expense ratio, evaluate risk factors, select the right lender, and prepare clear documentation. By following this process, you can approach each loan with confidence and consistency.

Ultimately, advanced bank statement mortgage loan structuring is about creating solutions. It is about seeing possibilities where others see obstacles. It is about understanding that every borrower's financial situation is unique and requires a tailored approach. When you master these principles, you gain the ability to turn challenging files into successful closings, build stronger relationships with clients, and establish yourself as an expert in the field.

This chapter lays the groundwork for everything that follows. As you move deeper into this book, you will build on these concepts and learn how to apply them in increasingly complex scenarios. The more you practice and refine these skills, the more natural they will become, and the more successful you will be in navigating the world of bank statement mortgage lending at the highest level.

Real-Life Math Example: Advanced Structuring of a Bank Statement Mortgage Loan

Consider a self-employed borrower who owns a marketing agency and is looking to purchase a primary residence. The borrower does not qualify using traditional tax returns due to significant business write-offs but has strong bank statement deposits. The borrower provides 12 months of business bank statements showing total deposits of $480,000 over the year. At first glance, this suggests an average monthly deposit of $40,000. However, advanced structuring requires a deeper analysis.

Upon reviewing the bank statements, it is determined that $60,000 of the total deposits are transfers between accounts and one-time payments that should not be considered qualifying income. After removing these non-recurring deposits, the adjusted total deposits are $420,000. This results in an average monthly deposit of $35,000. This step alone demonstrates the importance of accurate deposit analysis, as including non-qualifying deposits could lead to an inflated and unsustainable income calculation.

The next step is applying an expense ratio. The lender's standard expense factor is 50%, which would reduce the borrower's qualifying income to $17,500 per month. However, the borrower provides a CPA-prepared profit and loss statement showing that their actual business expenses are closer to 30%. By using this lower expense ratio, the qualifying income increases to $24,500 per month. This adjustment significantly improves the borrower's ability to qualify for a higher loan amount.

With a qualifying income of $24,500 per month, the next step is to calculate the maximum allowable housing payment. Assuming a conservative debt-to-income ratio of 50%, the borrower can allocate up to $12,250 per month toward housing expenses. This includes principal, interest, taxes, insurance, and any applicable association dues. If the borrower has minimal additional debt, most of this amount can be used for the mortgage payment.

Now consider the impact of loan structuring. At an interest rate of 7% on a 30-year fixed mortgage, a monthly payment of $12,250 supports a loan amount of approximately $1.85 million. However, this assumes no adjustments for risk factors. If the borrower has a credit score of 680, the lender may require a slightly lower debt-to-income ratio or a higher reserve requirement. By increasing the down payment from

10% to 20%, the borrower reduces the loan-to-value ratio, which can offset the credit risk and maintain the higher loan amount. Additionally, the borrower has $300,000 in liquid reserves after the down payment. This equates to more than 12 months of mortgage payments, which serves as a strong compensating factor. The presence of these reserves reassures the lender that the borrower can sustain the loan even during periods of lower income.

Now consider an alternative scenario where the borrower initially applied with only 12 months of statements showing inconsistent income. By waiting three months and providing updated statements with stronger deposits, the average monthly income increases from $35,000 to $38,000. This results in a higher qualifying income after applying the expense ratio, which in turn increases the maximum loan amount.

Another structuring option involves using a combination of personal and business bank statements. If the borrower transfers income from the business account to a personal account regularly, those personal deposits may reflect net income after expenses. In some cases, using personal bank statements can eliminate the need for an expense ratio altogether, further increasing qualifying income.

Through this example, you can see how multiple variables—deposit analysis, expense ratios, lender selection, credit profile, reserves, and timing—work together to shape the outcome of a loan. A less experienced professional might simply apply a standard 50% expense ratio and submit the file, resulting in a lower qualifying income and a potential denial. An advanced professional, however, evaluates every aspect of the file and makes strategic adjustments to maximize approval potential.

This is the essence of advanced bank statement mortgage loan structuring. It is not about manipulating numbers—it is about understanding the guidelines, using them effectively, and presenting a clear, accurate, and compelling financial picture. When done correctly, it allows borrowers who might otherwise be denied to achieve their goals and secure financing that aligns with their true financial capacity.

As you continue through this book, you will encounter more complex scenarios and deeper strategies that build on this foundation. Each example will reinforce the idea that success in this field comes from knowledge, attention to detail, and the ability to think strategically.

Chapter 2

Engineering Income Through Advanced Deposit Analysis and Account Strategy

At the advanced level of bank statement mortgage loan structuring, income is no longer something you simply calculate—it is something you engineer. This does not mean manipulating numbers or misrepresenting a borrower's financial situation. Instead, it means understanding how income is derived, how it is interpreted by lenders, and how to present it in the most accurate and advantageous way possible. The foundation of this process lies in advanced deposit analysis and strategic account selection, two skills that separate average loan submissions from consistently approved, high-quality files.

Most loan professionals begin by looking at total deposits and dividing them over a set period, typically 12 or 24 months. While this approach may produce a basic income figure, it often overlooks critical details that can either strengthen or weaken a file. Advanced deposit analysis requires a deeper examination of the borrower's financial behavior. It involves identifying patterns, distinguishing between recurring and non-recurring deposits, and understanding the nature of the borrower's business or income source.

Recurring deposits are the backbone of qualifying income. These are consistent inflows that reflect ongoing business activity or revenue generation. For example, a consultant who receives regular payments from clients, or a contractor who invoices monthly for services, will show a pattern of deposits that can be relied upon. Identifying these patterns allows you to build a stable and credible income profile. On the other hand, non-recurring deposits such as tax refunds, loan proceeds, asset sales, or internal transfers must be carefully evaluated and often excluded. Including these deposits can inflate income artificially and create issues during underwriting.

One of the most advanced aspects of deposit analysis is understanding the borrower's business model. Not all businesses generate income in the same way. Some operate on high volume with low margins, while others generate fewer but larger transactions. Seasonal businesses may have fluctuating income throughout the year, with certain months significantly stronger than others. Advanced structuring requires you to interpret these patterns and determine how best to present them. In some cases, using 24 months of statements can smooth out fluctuations, while in others, focusing on the most recent 12 months can highlight a positive trend.

Account selection plays a critical role in this process. Borrowers often have multiple accounts, including business checking, business savings, personal checking, and even secondary accounts used for specific purposes. Each account provides a different perspective on the borrower's financial activity. Business accounts typically reflect gross revenue, which requires the application of an expense ratio. Personal accounts, on the other hand, may show net income after expenses, potentially eliminating the need for an expense factor altogether.

Choosing the right accounts to use is both an art and a science. In some cases, using only business accounts provides the highest income, especially when a favorable expense ratio can be justified. In other cases, personal accounts offer a cleaner and more straightforward income calculation. There are also scenarios where combining accounts creates the most accurate representation of the borrower's income. This might involve using business accounts to demonstrate revenue and personal accounts to confirm consistent withdrawals or owner distributions.

Another advanced strategy involves isolating income streams within a single account. Many borrowers deposit multiple types of income into the same account, including business revenue, personal transfers, and other sources of funds. By carefully analyzing deposit descriptions, amounts, and frequencies, you can separate qualifying income from non-qualifying funds. This level of detail not only improves the accuracy of the income calculation but also strengthens the credibility of the file.

Documentation is essential when performing advanced deposit analysis. Underwriters need to understand how you arrived at your income calculation, and this requires clear and well-organized support. This may include deposit summaries, spreadsheets, and written explanations that outline your methodology. The goal is to make the underwriter's job as easy as possible by presenting a logical and transparent analysis.

Another key concept is consistency. Lenders are not just evaluating the amount of income—they are evaluating how reliable that income is over time. Large fluctuations or irregular deposit patterns can raise concerns, even if the overall income is strong. Advanced structuring involves identifying these inconsistencies and addressing them proactively. This might include providing explanations for seasonal variations, highlighting long-term growth trends, or excluding outlier months that do not accurately represent the borrower's typical income.

Timing also plays a significant role in deposit analysis. The selection of the time frame—whether 12 or 24 months—can have a substantial impact on the income calculation. In some cases, waiting for additional months of stronger deposits can improve the average income. In other cases, using a shorter time frame can highlight recent growth. Understanding when to proceed and when to wait is a strategic decision that can influence the outcome of the loan.

Advanced deposit analysis also involves understanding how different lenders interpret the same data. Some lenders are more conservative and may require stricter documentation or higher expense ratios. Others are more flexible and may allow for alternative approaches. By tailoring your analysis to the specific guidelines of the lender, you can increase the likelihood of approval and reduce the risk of delays or conditions.

Another important aspect is the treatment of large deposits. Large or irregular deposits can trigger additional scrutiny during underwriting. These deposits must be sourced and explained to ensure they are not considered borrowed funds or non-recurring income. Advanced structuring involves identifying these deposits early and preparing the necessary documentation to support them. This might include invoices, contracts, or other evidence that ties the deposit to legitimate business activity.

As you develop your skills in advanced deposit analysis, you will begin to see opportunities that others might miss. You will be able to identify which deposits strengthen the file and which should be excluded. You will understand how to present income in a way that aligns with lender expectations while accurately reflecting the borrower's financial reality. This ability to engineer income through careful analysis and strategic decision-making is one of the most valuable skills you can develop in the mortgage industry.

Ultimately, advanced deposit analysis is about creating clarity. It is about taking complex financial data and transforming it into a clear, consistent, and credible income story. When done correctly, it not only improves approval odds but also builds trust with underwriters and lenders. This trust can lead to smoother transactions, faster approvals, and stronger relationships over time.

As you continue through this book, you will build on these concepts and learn how to apply them in increasingly complex scenarios. The principles you learn here will serve as the foundation for advanced structuring strategies that can be applied across a wide range of borrower profiles and loan types.

Real-Life Math Example: Advanced Deposit Analysis and Account Structuring

Consider a self-employed borrower who owns a construction company and is applying for a bank statement mortgage loan. The borrower provides 24 months of bank statements from both a business account and a personal account. At first glance, the total deposits in the business account over the 24-month period are $1,200,000, which averages to $50,000 per month. However, advanced analysis reveals that not all deposits should be included in the income calculation.

Upon reviewing the statements, it is identified that $200,000 of the total deposits consist of internal transfers between accounts and occasional loan proceeds used to fund projects. These deposits are not considered qualifying income and must be excluded. After removing these non-recurring and non-qualifying deposits, the adjusted total deposits are $1,000,000 over 24 months, resulting in an average monthly deposit of approximately $41,667.

Next, the expense ratio is applied. The lender's standard expense factor for this type of business is 50%, which would reduce the qualifying income to approximately $20,833 per month. However, the borrower provides a CPA-prepared profit and loss statement showing that actual business expenses are closer to 35%. By using this lower expense ratio, the qualifying income increases to approximately $27,083 per month. This difference of over $6,000 per month in qualifying income can significantly impact the borrower's purchasing power. Now consider the personal account. The borrower regularly transfers funds from the business account to the personal account, resulting in total deposits of $600,000 over the same 24-month period. These deposits average $25,000 per month and represent net income after business expenses. In this case, the lender may allow the use of personal bank statements without applying an expense ratio, as the income has already been reduced by business expenses.

At this point, the loan professional must decide which approach results in the strongest file. Using the business account with a 35% expense ratio produces a qualifying income of $27,083 per month, while using the personal account produces a qualifying income of $25,000 per month. Although the business account provides slightly higher income, the personal account may offer a cleaner and more straightforward analysis with fewer documentation requirements.

To further refine the strategy, the loan professional analyzes the consistency of deposits in both accounts. The business account shows significant fluctuations, with some months exceeding $70,000 and others dropping below $30,000. The personal account, however, shows more consistent deposits ranging from $22,000 to $28,000 per month. This consistency may be viewed more favorably by the underwriter, even if the total income is slightly lower. Next, the borrower's debt obligations are considered. The borrower has monthly debts totaling $2,500, including auto loans and credit card payments. Using the personal account income of $25,000 per month, the maximum allowable housing expense at a 50% debt-to-income ratio would be $12,500. After subtracting existing debts, the borrower can allocate up to $10,000 per month toward housing expenses.

At an interest rate of 7%, a monthly payment of $10,000 supports a loan amount of approximately $1.5 million. If the borrower chooses to use the higher income from the business account, the maximum housing expense increases, potentially supporting a loan amount closer to $1.7 million. However, this comes with additional documentation requirements and potential scrutiny due to income fluctuations.

Now consider the impact of reserves. The borrower has $200,000 in liquid assets after the down payment. This provides approximately 12 months of reserves based on the projected housing payment, which strengthens the file and may allow for more flexibility in other areas such as credit or debt-to-income ratio.

Finally, timing is evaluated. The most recent six months of bank statements show stronger and more consistent deposits compared to earlier months. By waiting an additional three months and providing updated statements, the borrower's average monthly income could increase, further improving their qualifying profile.

Through this example, it becomes clear that advanced deposit analysis is not just about calculating income—it is about making strategic decisions that impact the overall strength of the loan file. By carefully evaluating deposits, selecting the appropriate accounts, applying the correct expense ratios, and considering factors such as consistency and timing, you can create a structured approach that maximizes approval potential.

This level of analysis allows you to move beyond basic calculations and into true loan engineering. It enables you to present a clear and compelling financial picture that aligns with lender guidelines while accurately reflecting the borrower's ability to repay the loan. As you continue to develop these skills, you will gain the confidence and expertise needed to handle even the most complex bank statement mortgage scenarios.

Chapter 3

Mastering Expense Ratios, CPA P&Ls, and Income Optimization Strategies

At the highest level of bank statement mortgage loan structuring, income is not only identified and analyzed—it is optimized. One of the most powerful tools for doing this is the strategic use of expense ratios and supporting documentation such as CPA-prepared profit and loss statements. While many loan professionals simply apply a standard expense factor and move forward, advanced structuring requires a deeper understanding of how expenses are interpreted, how they can be justified, and how they directly impact qualifying income.

Expense ratios represent the percentage of gross deposits that are assumed to be business expenses. For example, a lender applying a 50% expense ratio assumes that half of the borrower's deposits are used to cover business costs, leaving the remaining half as usable income. While this approach provides a quick and standardized method for calculating income, it often does not reflect the true financial performance of the borrower's business. Many businesses operate with significantly lower expenses, especially in service-based industries such as consulting, marketing, or online businesses. This is where advanced structuring begins to take shape.

Instead of accepting a default expense ratio, you begin to question whether that ratio accurately represents the borrower's business. If it does not, you look for ways to justify a lower expense factor. One of the most effective ways to do this is through a CPA-prepared profit and loss statement. A well-documented P&L can provide a detailed breakdown of revenue and expenses, allowing the lender to use actual expense data instead of a generalized assumption.

The impact of this adjustment can be substantial. Reducing an expense ratio from 50% to 30% increases qualifying income by 40%. This can mean the difference between a denial and an approval, or between a modest loan amount and a significantly larger one. However, using a CPA-prepared P&L requires more than simply providing the document. It must be consistent with the bank statements, supported by credible data, and presented in a way that aligns with lender expectations.

Consistency is one of the most critical factors when using a P&L. The income and expenses reported must reasonably match the deposits shown in the bank statements. Large discrepancies can raise concerns and lead to additional scrutiny or rejection of the document. Advanced structuring involves reviewing the P&L carefully, identifying any inconsistencies, and working with the borrower or CPA to ensure that the information is accurate and aligned. Another important consideration is the type of business the borrower operates. Different industries have different expense profiles. A construction company may have higher expenses due to materials and labor, while a digital marketing agency may have minimal overhead. Understanding these differences allows you to determine whether a lower expense ratio is reasonable and justifiable. It also helps you anticipate how the underwriter will view the file and what level of documentation will be required.

In some cases, lenders may allow a hybrid approach that combines bank statement analysis with a P&L. For example, the lender may use bank statements to verify revenue and a P&L to determine actual expenses. This approach can provide a more accurate representation of the borrower's income while still maintaining the flexibility of a bank statement loan. Advanced professionals understand how to leverage these options to achieve the best possible outcome.

Another strategy involves identifying and excluding certain expenses that are not relevant to the borrower's ability to repay the loan. For example, some business owners may have one-time expenses or investments that temporarily reduce their net income. By identifying these items and providing explanations or documentation, you can present a more accurate picture of the borrower's ongoing income. This requires careful analysis and clear communication with the lender. Depreciation is another factor that can impact income calculations. While depreciation reduces taxable income, it is a non-cash expense and does not affect the borrower's actual cash flow. In traditional mortgage underwriting, depreciation is often added back to income. In bank statement loans, this concept is less direct but still relevant when using a P&L. Understanding how to account for non-cash expenses can further optimize qualifying income.

Advanced structuring also involves understanding lender overlays. Some lenders may have minimum expense ratios that cannot be reduced, regardless of documentation. Others may require specific formats or certifications for P&Ls. Knowing these requirements in advance allows you to select the right lender and avoid unnecessary delays. It also ensures that your structuring strategy aligns with the lender's guidelines.

Another key concept is income layering. This involves combining multiple sources of income to strengthen the overall file. For example, a borrower may have business income from bank statements, rental income from investment properties, and additional income from side ventures. By carefully analyzing and combining these sources, you can create a more robust income profile that supports a higher loan amount. Risk management is also an important part of income optimization. While increasing qualifying income is beneficial, it must be done within the boundaries of lender guidelines and reasonable assumptions. Overstating income or relying on weak documentation can lead to issues during underwriting or even after closing. Advanced structuring involves finding the balance between maximizing income and maintaining credibility.

Another factor to consider is the borrower's long-term financial stability. Lenders are not just evaluating whether the borrower can qualify today—they are assessing whether the borrower can sustain the loan over time. This means that income must be consistent, reliable, and supported by a stable business or employment history. Advanced professionals take this into account when structuring the file and avoid strategies that may appear aggressive or unsustainable.

Communication with the borrower is also critical during this process. Borrowers may not fully understand how their financial decisions impact their ability to qualify for a loan. By educating them on the importance of clean deposits, consistent income, and proper documentation, you can help them position themselves more effectively. This not only improves the current loan but also sets them up for future opportunities.

As you continue to develop your expertise, you will begin to see expense ratios and P&Ls not as fixed constraints, but as variables that can be adjusted and optimized. You will understand when to accept a standard expense factor and when to challenge it. You will know how to present documentation that supports your analysis and builds confidence with the lender.

Ultimately, mastering expense ratios and income optimization strategies allows you to unlock the full potential of bank statement loans. It gives you the ability to serve a wider range of borrowers, close more complex deals, and achieve better outcomes for your clients. This chapter provides the foundation for these skills, which will be expanded upon in the chapters that follow.

Real-Life Math Example: Optimizing Income Using Expense Ratios and CPA P&L

Consider a self-employed borrower who owns an online consulting business and is applying for a bank statement mortgage loan. The borrower provides 12 months of business bank statements showing total deposits of $360,000, which averages to $30,000 per month. At first glance, this appears to be a strong income profile. However, the way expenses are calculated will determine the borrower's qualifying income.

Using the lender's standard expense ratio of 50%, the qualifying income would be reduced to $15,000 per month. Based on a maximum debt-to-income ratio of 50%, the borrower could allocate up to $7,500 per month toward housing expenses. After accounting for existing debts of $1,500 per month, the borrower would have $6,000 available for a mortgage payment. At an interest rate of 7%, this supports a loan amount of approximately $900,000.

However, the borrower provides a CPA-prepared profit and loss statement showing that actual business expenses are only 25% of revenue. This means that the borrower's net income is 75% of deposits, or $22,500 per month. This represents a significant increase from the $15,000 calculated using the standard expense ratio.

With a qualifying income of $22,500 per month, the maximum housing expense at a 50% debt-to-income ratio increases to $11,250. After subtracting the borrower's existing debts of $1,500, the borrower can now allocate $9,750 per month toward housing. At the same interest rate of 7%, this supports a loan amount of approximately $1.45 million.

This single adjustment—using a CPA-prepared P&L to justify a lower expense ratio—increases the borrower's purchasing power by over $500,000. This demonstrates the power of advanced income optimization and the importance of accurate expense analysis. Now consider an additional layer of structuring. The borrower also has a rental property that generates $2,000 per month in net income. By adding this income to the borrower's qualifying income, the total monthly income increases to $24,500. This further increases the maximum allowable housing expense and supports an even higher loan amount.

Next, the borrower's reserves are evaluated. The borrower has $150,000 in liquid assets after the down payment, which provides approximately 12 months of reserves based on the projected mortgage payment. This strong reserve position serves as a compensating factor and may allow for more flexibility in other areas such as credit or debt-to-income ratio.

Now consider the impact of timing. The borrower's most recent three months of bank statements show higher deposits, averaging $35,000 per month. By waiting to include these months in the calculation, the borrower's average income increases, further improving their qualifying profile.

Another consideration is lender selection. Some lenders may accept the CPA-prepared P&L and allow the lower expense ratio, while others may require the standard 50% factor. By choosing a lender that supports the borrower's actual expense profile, the loan professional can maximize the borrower's qualifying income and improve approval odds. Through this example, it becomes clear that expense ratios and P&Ls are not just technical details—they are powerful tools that can significantly impact the outcome of a loan. By understanding how to use these tools effectively, you can create a structured approach that maximizes income while maintaining accuracy and credibility.

This level of analysis and strategy is what defines advanced bank statement mortgage loan structuring. It allows you to go beyond basic calculations and create customized solutions that align with both borrower needs and lender requirements. As you continue to build on these concepts, you will gain the expertise needed to handle even the most complex loan scenarios with confidence and precision.

Chapter 4

Risk Layering, Compensating Factors, and Structuring for Approval

At the advanced level of bank statement mortgage loan structuring, success is no longer determined by a single factor such as income or credit score. Instead, it is the result of how multiple elements within a loan file interact with one another. This concept is known as risk layering. Every loan carries some level of risk, and lenders evaluate that risk by analyzing a combination of factors including income stability, credit history, loan-to-value ratio, reserves, property type, and borrower experience. Advanced structuring is the process of balancing these factors in a way that transforms a potentially weak file into a strong and approvable one.

Risk layering begins with understanding that no file is perfect. Even high-income borrowers may have credit issues. Strong credit borrowers may have inconsistent income. Investors may have complex property portfolios that introduce additional risk. The key is not to eliminate all risk, but to offset weaknesses with strengths. This is where compensating factors come into play. A compensating factor is any positive element in the loan file that reduces the lender's perceived risk and increases the likelihood of approval. One of the most powerful compensating factors is a lower loan-to-value ratio. When a borrower contributes a larger down payment or has significant equity in a refinance, the lender's exposure is reduced. This makes the loan more attractive, even if other aspects of the file are less than ideal. For example, a borrower with a 660 credit score may still be approved if they are putting down 30% instead of 10%. Advanced structuring involves identifying opportunities to adjust the loan structure in ways that improve LTV and reduce overall risk.

Reserves are another critical compensating factor. Lenders want to know that borrowers have the ability to continue making payments even if their income fluctuates. This is especially important for self-employed borrowers, whose income may not be as predictable as that of a salaried employee. Demonstrating strong reserves—often measured in months of mortgage payments—can significantly strengthen a file. Advanced professionals understand how to document and present reserves in a way that highlights the borrower's financial stability.

Credit is another key component of risk layering. While bank statement loans are more flexible than traditional loans, credit still plays an important role in underwriting decisions. A higher credit score can offset weaknesses in other areas, while a lower score may require stronger compensating factors.

Advanced structuring involves not only evaluating the borrower's current credit profile but also identifying opportunities for improvement. This might include paying down balances, correcting errors on the credit report, or waiting for a recent credit event to season further.

Income consistency is closely tied to risk perception. Even if a borrower has strong average income, significant fluctuations can raise concerns. Lenders prefer stable and predictable income streams. Advanced structuring involves identifying patterns in the borrower's income and presenting them in a way that emphasizes consistency. This might include using a longer time frame to smooth out fluctuations or providing explanations for irregularities.

Property type and occupancy also influence risk. Owner-occupied properties are generally considered lower risk than investment properties, while certain property types such as multi-unit properties or short-term rentals may carry additional scrutiny. Advanced structuring involves understanding how these factors impact the overall risk profile and adjusting other elements of the file accordingly. For example, a borrower purchasing an investment property may need stronger reserves or a lower LTV to offset the increased risk. Another important concept is borrower experience. For investment properties, lenders often consider whether the borrower has prior experience managing similar properties. A seasoned investor with a track record of successful property management may be viewed more favorably than a first-time investor. Advanced structuring involves highlighting relevant experience and demonstrating the borrower's ability to manage the property effectively.

Debt-to-income ratio, or DTI, is another key factor in risk layering. While bank statement loans often allow higher DTIs than traditional loans, there are still limits. Advanced structuring involves managing DTI by adjusting income, reducing debt, or restructuring the loan. This might include paying off certain debts, consolidating obligations, or selecting a loan program with more flexible DTI guidelines.

Timing is also a critical component of risk management. The timing of the loan application can impact multiple aspects of the file, including income, credit, and reserves. For example, waiting for a credit score to improve or for additional reserves to be accumulated can strengthen the file significantly. Advanced professionals understand how to evaluate timing and make strategic decisions that improve the borrower's position.

Another advanced strategy is layering multiple compensating factors simultaneously. Instead of relying on a single strength, you combine several elements to create a strong overall profile. For example, a borrower with moderate credit may still be approved if they have strong income, low LTV, and significant reserves. Each of these factors contributes to reducing the lender's perceived risk, making the loan more acceptable.

Communication and presentation are essential in risk layering. The way a file is presented can influence how it is perceived by the underwriter. A well-organized file with clear explanations and supporting documentation can make a significant difference. Advanced structuring involves not only building a strong file but also presenting it in a way that highlights its strengths and addresses potential concerns.

Another important aspect is anticipating underwriting questions. Experienced professionals can identify potential issues before the file is submitted and address them proactively. This might include providing explanations for large deposits, documenting the source of funds, or clarifying inconsistencies in the borrower's financial history. By addressing these issues upfront, you reduce the likelihood of delays or conditions during underwriting.

As you develop your skills in risk layering, you will begin to see each loan file as a dynamic system rather than a static set of numbers. You will understand how changes in one area can impact the overall profile and how to adjust multiple variables to achieve the desired outcome. This level of insight allows you to approach complex files with confidence and creativity.

Ultimately, mastering risk layering and compensating factors is about creating balance. It is about understanding that no file is perfect and that success comes from strategically combining strengths to offset weaknesses. When done correctly, this approach not only increases approval rates but also allows you to serve a broader range of borrowers and close more complex deals.

This chapter provides the framework for understanding and applying these concepts. As you continue through this book, you will build on this foundation and learn how to apply risk layering strategies in increasingly sophisticated scenarios.

Real-Life Math Example: Structuring a High-Risk File Using Compensating Factors

Consider a self-employed borrower who is applying for a bank statement mortgage loan to purchase an investment property. The borrower provides 12 months of bank statements showing average monthly deposits of $25,000. After applying a 40% expense ratio, the qualifying income is $15,000 per month. At first glance, this appears sufficient to support a mortgage.

However, the borrower has several risk factors that must be addressed.

The borrower's credit score is 660, which is considered moderate risk. Additionally, the borrower is purchasing an investment property, which carries higher risk than a primary residence. The borrower also has limited reserves, with only $50,000 remaining after the down payment. These factors combined create a challenging file that may not be approved without advanced structuring.

The first step is to evaluate the borrower's debt-to-income ratio. The borrower has existing monthly debts of $3,000. Using a maximum DTI of 50%, the borrower can allocate up to $7,500 per month toward housing expenses. After subtracting existing debts, the borrower has $4,500 available for a mortgage payment. At an interest rate of 7.5%, this supports a loan amount of approximately $600,000.

However, the lender's guidelines for investment properties with a 660 credit score may limit the maximum LTV to 75%. This means that for a $600,000 loan, the property value must be at least $800,000, requiring a down payment of $200,000. If the borrower initially planned to put down only 20%, this would not meet the lender's requirements.

To strengthen the file, the borrower decides to increase the down payment to 25%, reducing the loan amount and improving the LTV. This adjustment not only meets the lender's guidelines but also reduces the monthly payment, lowering the DTI. With a lower loan amount of $550,000, the monthly payment decreases to approximately $4,100, which fits within the borrower's allowable housing expense.

Next, the borrower addresses the reserve requirement. The lender requires at least six months of reserves for investment properties, but the borrower's current reserves are insufficient. To resolve this, the borrower moves additional funds from a brokerage account, increasing total reserves to $100,000. This provides more than 12 months of reserves based on the projected mortgage payment, significantly strengthening the file.

Another adjustment involves improving the borrower's credit profile. By paying down credit card balances and correcting a reporting error, the borrower is able to increase their credit score from 660 to 680. This improvement may allow for more favorable terms and slightly higher flexibility in other areas.

Now consider the impact of these changes. The borrower's improved credit score, lower LTV, and increased reserves all serve as compensating factors that offset the initial risks. The lender is now more likely to approve the loan, even with the higher-risk property type and moderate income. Additionally, the loan professional prepares a detailed loan summary that explains the borrower's business, income stability, and investment experience. This narrative helps the underwriter understand the borrower's overall profile and reduces uncertainty.

Through this example, it becomes clear that advanced structuring is not about changing the borrower's financial situation—it is about presenting it in the most effective way possible. By adjusting variables such as down payment, reserves, and credit, and by clearly communicating the strengths of the file, you can transform a challenging loan into an approvable one.

This is the power of risk layering and compensating factors. It allows you to take control of the loan process and create outcomes that might not be possible through a basic, one-dimensional approach. As you continue to develop these skills, you will gain the ability to navigate even the most complex loan scenarios with confidence and precision.

Chapter 5

Lender Selection, Investor Overlays, and Strategic Program Matching

At the advanced level of bank statement mortgage loan structuring, one of the most overlooked yet powerful skills is lender selection. Many loan professionals focus heavily on income calculations, documentation, and borrower qualifications, but fail to recognize that the same borrower can receive completely different outcomes depending on which lender the loan is submitted to. This is because every lender operates under its own set of guidelines, risk tolerances, and investor overlays. Understanding these differences—and knowing how to match a borrower to the right program—is one of the most important aspects of advanced structuring.

Investor overlays are additional guidelines imposed by lenders that go beyond standard program requirements. While many lenders may offer bank statement loan programs, they do not all interpret or apply the guidelines in the same way. Some lenders are more conservative, requiring higher credit scores, lower debt-to-income ratios, or stricter documentation. Others are more flexible, allowing for higher DTIs, lower credit scores, or alternative forms of income verification. Advanced structuring involves identifying these differences and using them to your advantage.

The first step in strategic lender selection is understanding the borrower's profile in detail. This includes income, credit, reserves, property type, loan purpose, and overall financial stability. Each of these factors interacts with lender guidelines in different ways. For example, a borrower with strong income but lower credit may be better suited for a lender that prioritizes income over credit score. Conversely, a borrower with excellent credit but variable income may benefit from a lender that offers more flexibility in income calculation.

One of the most critical areas where lenders differ is in their approach to expense ratios. Some lenders apply a flat expense factor, such as 50%, regardless of the borrower's business type. Others allow for reduced expense ratios based on documentation such as CPA-prepared profit and loss statements. Choosing a lender that allows for a lower expense ratio can significantly increase qualifying income and improve approval odds.

Another key difference is how lenders treat personal versus business bank statements. Some lenders prefer business accounts and require the application of an expense ratio, while others allow personal accounts to be used without applying an expense factor. This distinction can have a major impact on the borrower's qualifying income. Advanced professionals understand how to evaluate both options and select the lender that provides the most favorable outcome.

Debt-to-income ratio limits also vary between lenders. While some lenders cap DTI at 43% or 45%, others may allow DTIs up to 50% or higher, especially when strong compensating factors are present. For borrowers who are close to the DTI limit, selecting a lender with more flexible guidelines can make the difference between approval and denial.

Credit score requirements are another area where lender selection is critical. Some lenders have minimum credit score requirements as low as 620, while others require 680 or higher. Additionally, lenders may have different pricing adjustments based on credit score tiers. Understanding these nuances allows you to position the borrower with the lender that offers the best combination of approval likelihood and loan terms.

Loan-to-value limits also differ across lenders. For example, one lender may allow up to 90% LTV on a primary residence, while another may cap LTV at 80% for the same borrower profile. For investment properties, the differences can be even more pronounced. Advanced structuring involves evaluating these limits and adjusting the loan structure accordingly.

Reserves requirements are another important consideration. Some lenders require a minimum number of months of reserves based on the property type and loan amount. Others may have more flexible requirements, especially for borrowers with strong income or credit. By selecting a lender with more favorable reserve requirements, you can improve the borrower's chances of approval.

Another key factor is how lenders treat unique borrower scenarios. For example, some lenders are more accommodating of recent credit events such as bankruptcies or foreclosures, while others require longer seasoning periods. Some lenders are more experienced with self-employed borrowers and have streamlined processes for evaluating complex income. Understanding these differences allows you to match the borrower with the lender that is best equipped to handle their specific situation.

Turnaround time and underwriting efficiency are also important considerations. A lender with faster processing times and more responsive underwriting can provide a better overall experience for both the borrower and the loan professional. While this may not directly impact approval, it can influence the success of the transaction, especially in competitive markets.

Pricing is another factor that must be considered in lender selection. Interest rates, fees, and overall loan costs can vary significantly between lenders. Advanced structuring involves balancing approval likelihood with cost considerations to ensure that the borrower receives a competitive and sustainable loan.

Another advanced strategy is maintaining relationships with multiple lenders. By working with a variety of investors, you gain access to a broader range of programs and guidelines. This allows you to pivot quickly if a loan does not fit one lender's criteria and find an alternative solution without starting the process from scratch.

Pre-underwriting is another valuable tool in advanced lender selection. By reviewing the borrower's file in detail before submission and, in some cases, discussing it with the lender, you can identify potential issues and address them proactively. This reduces the likelihood of surprises during underwriting and increases the chances of a smooth approval process.

Communication is key throughout this process. Clearly presenting the borrower's profile, income calculation, and supporting documentation helps the lender understand the file and make informed decisions. A well-prepared submission not only improves approval odds but also builds trust with the lender. Another important concept is flexibility. Markets change, guidelines evolve, and borrower circumstances can shift. Advanced professionals remain adaptable, continuously updating their knowledge of lender programs and adjusting their strategies accordingly. This ability to adapt ensures that you can continue to provide effective solutions even as conditions change.

Ultimately, lender selection is about alignment. It is about finding the intersection between the borrower's profile and the lender's guidelines. When these elements are aligned, approvals become more consistent, transactions move more smoothly, and outcomes improve for everyone involved.

This chapter emphasizes that advanced structuring is not just about what is in the file—it is also about where the file is sent. By mastering lender selection and understanding investor overlays, you gain a powerful advantage that can significantly impact your success in the mortgage industry.

Real-Life Math Example: Matching a Borrower to the Optimal Lender

Consider a self-employed borrower who is applying for a bank statement mortgage loan to purchase a primary residence. The borrower provides 12 months of business bank statements showing total deposits of $300,000, which averages to

$25,000 per month. The borrower also has a credit score of 670, existing monthly debts of $2,000, and $80,000 in reserves after the down payment.

Using a standard expense ratio of 50%, the borrower's qualifying income would be $12,500 per month. At a maximum DTI of 45%, the borrower could allocate up to $5,625 toward housing expenses. After subtracting existing debts, the borrower would have $3,625 available for a mortgage payment. At an interest rate of 7%, this supports a loan amount of approximately $550,000.

However, this is only one possible outcome based on a specific lender's guidelines. Now consider a second lender that allows a reduced expense ratio of 30% with a CPA-prepared profit and loss statement. Using this lower expense ratio, the borrower's qualifying income increases to $17,500 per month. At a maximum DTI of 50%, the borrower can allocate up to $8,750 toward housing expenses. After subtracting existing debts, the borrower has $6,750 available for a mortgage payment.

At the same interest rate of 7%, this higher payment supports a loan amount of approximately $1 million. This represents a nearly $450,000 increase in purchasing power simply by selecting a different lender with more flexible guidelines.

Now consider a third lender that allows the use of personal bank statements without applying an expense ratio. The borrower provides personal bank statements showing average monthly deposits of $20,000, representing net income after expenses. Using this income, the borrower's qualifying income is $20,000 per month. At a 50% DTI, the borrower can allocate $10,000 toward housing expenses. After subtracting existing debts, the borrower has $8,000 available for a mortgage payment.

At an interest rate of 7%, this supports a loan amount of approximately $1.2 million. This is the highest loan amount among the three options, but it may come with different documentation requirements or pricing considerations.

Next, consider the impact of credit score requirements. The borrower's credit score of 670 may qualify with all three lenders, but one lender may offer better pricing for borrowers with scores above 680. By improving the credit score slightly, the borrower could access more favorable terms, further improving the overall loan.

Reserves also play a role in lender selection. Some lenders may require only six months of reserves, while others may require twelve months for higher loan amounts. The borrower's

$80,000 in reserves may be sufficient for one lender but not for another, influencing the choice of program.

Through this example, it becomes clear that lender selection is not a one-size-fits-all decision. Each lender offers a different combination of guidelines, flexibility, and pricing. By analyzing these differences and matching them to the borrower's profile, you can significantly improve the outcome of the loan.

This example highlights the importance of viewing lender selection as a strategic decision rather than a default choice. By understanding how different lenders evaluate the same borrower, you can position the loan for maximum success and create opportunities that might otherwise be missed.

As you continue to develop your expertise, you will gain the ability to quickly identify the best lender for each scenario and adapt your strategy accordingly. This skill is a key component of advanced bank statement mortgage loan structuring and will play a critical role in your long-term success.

Chapter 6

Documentation Mastery, Narrative Framing, and Underwriter Psychology

At the advanced level of bank statement mortgage loan structuring, numbers alone are not enough. Even the most perfectly calculated income and well-balanced risk profile can fail if the documentation is unclear, inconsistent, or poorly presented. This is where documentation mastery and narrative framing become essential. Advanced professionals understand that underwriting is not just a mechanical process—it is a human process. Underwriters are tasked with evaluating risk, verifying accuracy, and making judgment calls based on the information presented to them. The way a file is documented and explained can significantly influence the outcome.

Documentation mastery begins with organization. A well-structured file allows the underwriter to quickly understand the borrower's financial profile without confusion or unnecessary back-and-forth. This means clearly labeling bank statements, separating personal and business accounts, organizing deposits chronologically, and ensuring that all pages are complete and legible. Missing pages, inconsistent formatting, or unclear documentation can create doubt and slow down the process. Beyond organization, clarity is critical.

Every number presented in the income calculation must be supported by documentation that is easy to follow. If deposits are excluded, the reasoning should be documented. If an expense ratio is reduced, the supporting evidence should be clearly presented. Advanced structuring involves anticipating questions before they are asked and providing answers within the file itself.

This is where narrative framing comes into play. A loan file is more than a collection of documents—it is a story. The borrower's financial profile, business activity, and income patterns must be presented in a way that makes sense to the underwriter. A strong narrative explains how the borrower earns income, why certain deposits are included or excluded, and how the overall financial picture supports the ability to repay the loan.

For example, a borrower with fluctuating income may initially appear risky. However, if the narrative explains that the borrower operates a seasonal business with predictable peak periods, and this pattern is supported by historical data, the underwriter may view the file more favorably. The key is to provide context that transforms raw data into a clear and logical story.

One of the most effective tools for narrative framing is the loan summary. This document provides an overview of the borrower's profile, including income calculation, business description, credit profile, and compensating factors. A well-written loan summary guides the underwriter through the file and highlights the strengths of the borrower. It also addresses potential concerns upfront, reducing the likelihood of conditions or delays.

Underwriter psychology is an important aspect of advanced structuring. Underwriters are trained to identify risk, but they are also looking for reasons to approve loans that meet guidelines. When a file is clear, consistent, and well-documented, it builds confidence and makes the underwriter's job easier. Conversely, a disorganized or unclear file can create uncertainty, even if the borrower technically qualifies.

Consistency across documents is one of the most important factors in building this confidence. The borrower's stated income should align with bank statement deposits, business activity, and any supporting documentation such as a CPA-prepared profit and loss statement. Discrepancies can raise red flags and lead to additional scrutiny. Advanced professionals carefully review all documents to ensure alignment before submission.

Another key aspect is the handling of large or unusual deposits. These deposits often trigger conditions during underwriting and must be explained. Advanced structuring involves identifying these deposits early, determining their source, and providing documentation such as invoices, contracts, or written explanations. By addressing these items upfront, you reduce the likelihood of delays and demonstrate thoroughness.

Business verification is another important component of documentation. Lenders want to confirm that the borrower's business is legitimate and active. This may include verifying business licenses, online presence, or third-party documentation. Ensuring that this information is accurate and consistent with the borrower's stated income helps strengthen the file.

The presentation of bank statements is also critical. Statements should be complete, with all pages included, and should clearly show account holder information, account numbers, and transaction details. Highlighting or annotating key deposits can help the underwriter quickly identify relevant information. However, this should be done carefully to avoid creating confusion.

Another advanced strategy is creating a deposit summary or

income worksheet. This document outlines how income was calculated, including total deposits, excluded items, and the application of any expense ratio. By providing a clear breakdown, you make it easier for the underwriter to verify your calculations and understand your methodology.

Communication with the underwriter is also part of documentation mastery. While most communication occurs through the file itself, there are times when direct communication may be necessary. This might include clarifying a unique aspect of the borrower's business or addressing a specific condition. Maintaining a professional and collaborative approach helps build trust and facilitates smoother transactions.

Timing and sequencing of documentation can also impact the outcome. Submitting a complete and well-prepared file from the beginning reduces the need for additional conditions and speeds up the approval process. Advanced professionals take the time to gather all necessary documentation upfront rather than submitting incomplete files and reacting to conditions later.

Another important consideration is compliance. All documentation must meet lender and regulatory requirements. This includes ensuring that documents are authentic, properly signed, and free of alterations. Advanced structuring always operates within the boundaries of compliance, maintaining integrity while optimizing outcomes. Borrower education is also part of the process. Helping borrowers understand the importance of documentation and how their financial behavior impacts the loan can lead to better outcomes. For example, advising a borrower to avoid large unexplained deposits or to maintain consistent account activity can simplify the underwriting process.

As you develop your skills in documentation and narrative framing, you will begin to see how small details can have a significant impact. A well-organized file can turn a complex scenario into a straightforward approval, while a poorly presented file can create unnecessary challenges.

Ultimately, documentation mastery and underwriter psychology are about communication. They are about presenting information in a way that is clear, logical, and persuasive. When you combine strong documentation with a compelling narrative, you create a file that not only meets guidelines but also inspires confidence.

This chapter emphasizes that advanced structuring is not just about numbers—it is about presentation. By mastering documentation and understanding how underwriters think, you can significantly improve your approval rates and create a more efficient and successful loan process.

Real-Life Math Example: Structuring and Presenting a Complex File for Approval

Consider a self-employed borrower who owns a landscaping business and is applying for a bank statement mortgage loan to purchase a primary residence. The borrower provides 12 months of business bank statements showing total deposits of $240,000, averaging $20,000 per month. However, the deposits are inconsistent, with some months as high as $30,000 and others as low as $12,000.

The first step is to analyze the deposits and identify non-recurring items. Upon review, it is determined that $30,000 of the total deposits consist of transfers and one-time payments that should be excluded. This reduces the total qualifying deposits to $210,000, resulting in an average monthly deposit of $17,500.

Next, an expense ratio of 40% is applied, based on the nature of the business and supporting documentation. This results in a qualifying income of $10,500 per month. At a maximum debt-to-income ratio of 50%, the borrower can allocate up to $5,250 toward housing expenses. After subtracting existing debts of $1,250 per month, the borrower has $4,000 available for a mortgage payment. At an interest rate of 7%, this supports a loan amount of approximately $600,000. However, the borrower's income fluctuations and moderate credit score of 665 create potential concerns for the underwriter.

To address these concerns, the loan professional prepares a detailed income worksheet that outlines the deposit analysis, including excluded items and the application of the expense ratio. This document provides a clear and transparent calculation that the underwriter can easily verify.

Additionally, a loan summary is included that explains the borrower's business model. The summary highlights that the landscaping business is seasonal, with higher income during spring and summer months. Historical data is provided to show that this pattern is consistent year over year, reinforcing the stability of the borrower's income.

The borrower also provides documentation for several large deposits, including invoices and contracts that tie the deposits to legitimate business activity. This eliminates concerns about the source of funds and strengthens the credibility of the file.

To further improve the file, the borrower demonstrates $80,000 in reserves, which provides approximately 12 months of mortgage payments. This serves as a strong compensating factor and offsets the income variability.

The loan professional also ensures that all bank statements are complete, clearly labeled, and organized in chronological order. Key deposits are highlighted to make it easier for the underwriter to review the file.

Now consider the impact of this presentation. While the initial numbers may have raised concerns, the clear documentation and narrative framing transform the file into a well-supported and understandable case. The underwriter can see not only the borrower's income but also the context behind it.

Without this level of documentation and explanation, the file might have resulted in multiple conditions or even a denial. With it, the loan is more likely to be approved efficiently.

This example demonstrates that advanced structuring is not just about calculating income—it is about presenting that income in a way that aligns with lender expectations and builds confidence. By combining accurate calculations with strong documentation and narrative framing, you create a file that stands out and increases the likelihood of approval.

As you continue to refine these skills, you will gain the ability to handle increasingly complex scenarios and achieve consistent success in bank statement mortgage loan structuring.

Chapter 7

Timing, Sequencing, and Strategic Positioning for Maximum Approval

At the advanced level of bank statement mortgage loan structuring, one of the most powerful yet underestimated tools is timing. While income, credit, and documentation are essential, when you submit a loan can be just as important as how you structure it. Strategic timing and sequencing allow you to position a borrower at their strongest possible moment, maximizing approval odds, improving loan terms, and often increasing the loan amount. This chapter focuses on how to control timing, align key variables, and engineer the optimal moment for submission.

Most loan professionals operate reactively. A borrower applies, documents are collected, and the loan is submitted as quickly as possible. While speed can be important, it often comes at the cost of strength. Advanced professionals take a different approach. They evaluate whether the borrower is currently in the best possible position to qualify or whether a short delay could significantly improve the file. This shift from urgency to strategy is what separates average results from elite outcomes. The first element of timing is income positioning. Bank statement loans rely heavily on historical deposits, typically over 12 or 24 months. This means that each new month of statements has the potential to impact the average income calculation. If a borrower has recently experienced stronger income months, waiting to include those months in the analysis can increase qualifying income. Conversely, if recent months are weaker, it may be beneficial to move forward before those months are included.

For example, consider a borrower whose income has been steadily increasing over the past year. Submitting the loan using the most recent 12 months of statements may result in a higher average income than using an earlier period. Advanced structuring involves identifying these trends and selecting the time frame that produces the strongest result.

Credit timing is another critical factor. Credit scores can change based on recent activity, such as paying down balances, resolving collections, or correcting reporting errors. Even a small increase in credit score can move the borrower into a more favorable pricing tier or unlock access to better loan programs. Advanced professionals evaluate whether it makes sense to improve credit before submitting the loan and guide the borrower through the necessary steps.

Debt reduction is closely tied to both timing and sequencing. Paying off or reducing certain debts before applying can improve the borrower's debt-to-income ratio, increasing the amount they can qualify for. However, this must be done strategically. For example, paying off a large installment loan may have a different impact than reducing revolving credit balances. Understanding how different types of debt affect underwriting allows you to make informed decisions.

Reserve accumulation is another area where timing can make a significant difference. Lenders often require a certain number of months of reserves based on the loan amount and property type. If a borrower is close to meeting these requirements, waiting to accumulate additional funds can strengthen the file. This is particularly important for higher-risk scenarios such as investment properties or jumbo loans.

Another key concept is sequencing financial actions in the correct order. For example, if a borrower plans to move funds between accounts, pay down debt, or make large deposits, the timing of these actions can impact how they are viewed during underwriting. Large, unexplained deposits can create issues, so it is often better to complete these transactions well in advancc of thc application and allow them to season.

Seasoning refers to the period of time that funds or financial changes must be reflected in the borrower's accounts before they are considered stable and acceptable by lenders. Understanding seasoning requirements allows you to plan ahead and avoid potential issues. For example, funds that have been in an account for several months are generally viewed more favorably than recently deposited funds.

Another advanced timing strategy involves aligning multiple variables simultaneously. Instead of improving one aspect of the file, you coordinate improvements across income, credit, reserves, and documentation. For example, a borrower might wait three months to include stronger bank statement deposits, pay down credit card balances to increase their score, and accumulate additional reserves. When these improvements are combined, the overall impact can be substantial.

Market conditions also play a role in timing. Interest rates, lender guidelines, and program availability can change over time. While these factors are not always predictable, staying informed about market trends allows you to make better decisions. For example, if rates are expected to increase, it may be beneficial to move forward sooner. If new programs or guideline changes are anticipated, waiting may provide additional opportunities.

Another important aspect of timing is borrower readiness. Some borrowers are eager to move forward immediately, while others may benefit from a period of preparation. Advanced professionals take the time to evaluate readiness and provide guidance on how to improve the borrower's position. This might include recommendations on managing bank accounts, avoiding large unexplained deposits, or maintaining consistent income patterns.

Communication is essential throughout this process. Borrowers need to understand why timing matters and how their actions impact the outcome of the loan. By educating them on these concepts, you can align expectations and ensure that they are actively participating in the structuring process.

Another critical factor is avoiding rushed submissions. Submitting a loan before it is fully optimized can lead to unnecessary conditions, delays, or even denial. Advanced professionals prioritize preparation over speed, ensuring that the file is as strong as possible before it is submitted.

Pre-underwriting can also be used as a timing tool. By reviewing the file internally or with the lender before formal submission, you can identify potential issues and address them proactively. This allows you to refine the file and improve its chances of approval.

Flexibility is key when it comes to timing. Each borrower's situation is unique, and there is no one-size-fits-all approach. Advanced structuring involves evaluating all variables and determining the optimal strategy based on the specific circumstances.

As you develop your skills in timing and sequencing, you will begin to see opportunities to improve files that might otherwise appear marginal. You will understand how small adjustments in timing can lead to significant improvements in outcomes. This ability to control the timing of a loan is a powerful tool that can dramatically increase your success rate.

Ultimately, timing and sequencing are about positioning. They are about ensuring that the borrower is presented to the lender at their strongest possible moment. When combined with the other advanced strategies in this series, they allow you to consistently achieve high-level results and navigate complex scenarios with confidence.

Real-Life Math Example: Using Timing and Sequencing to Increase Loan Approval Power

Consider a self-employed borrower who owns a fitness coaching business and is applying for a bank statement mortgage loan. The borrower provides 12 months of bank statements showing total deposits of $300,000, averaging

$25,000 per month. After applying a 50% expense ratio, the qualifying income is $12,500 per month. The borrower has existing monthly debts of $2,500, and the lender allows a maximum debt-to-income ratio of 50%. This means the borrower can allocate up to $6,250 toward housing expenses. After subtracting existing debts, the borrower has $3,750 available for a mortgage payment. At an interest rate of 7%, this supports a loan amount of approximately $575,000.

However, a closer analysis reveals that the borrower's income has increased significantly in recent months. The most recent three months show deposits of $35,000, $38,000, and $40,000. If the borrower waits three months and includes these higher-income months in the calculation, the average monthly deposits increase.

After recalculating with the updated 12-month period, the total deposits rise to $360,000, resulting in an average of $30,000 per month. Applying the same 50% expense ratio, the qualifying income increases to $15,000 per month.

With this higher income, the maximum housing expense at a 50% DTI increases to $7,500. After subtracting existing debts of $2,500, the borrower now has $5,000 available for a mortgage payment. At the same interest rate of 7%, this supports a loan amount of approximately $750,000—an increase of $175,000 compared to the original scenario.

Now consider the impact of credit improvement. The borrower's current credit score is 665. By paying down credit card balances and correcting a reporting error, the borrower increases their score to 685. This improvement may allow for better pricing and slightly higher flexibility in DTI or LTV requirements.

Next, the borrower addresses reserves. Initially, the borrower has $40,000 in reserves, which may be borderline for the desired loan amount. By waiting and saving an additional $20,000, the borrower increases total reserves to $60,000, providing a stronger financial profile.

Now consider the combined impact of these changes. The borrower's higher income, improved credit score, and increased reserves all contribute to a stronger file. The loan professional can now position the borrower for a larger loan amount with better terms and a higher likelihood of approval.

Additionally, the borrower avoids making large, unexplained deposits during this period, ensuring that the bank statements remain clean and easy to analyze. This reduces the risk of conditions during underwriting.

Through this example, it becomes clear that timing and sequencing can have a profound impact on the outcome of a loan. By waiting for stronger income months, improving credit, and increasing reserves, the borrower significantly improves their qualifying profile. This approach demonstrates that advanced structuring is not just about working with what is available today—it is about planning for a better outcome tomorrow. By understanding how timing affects each component of the loan, you can create strategies that maximize approval potential and deliver better results for your clients.

As you continue to refine these skills, you will gain the ability to identify the optimal timing for each loan and guide borrowers through the steps needed to achieve the best possible outcome.

Chapter 8

Cash-Out Strategies, Liquidity Engineering, and Using Bank Statement Loans to Unlock Equity

At the advanced level of bank statement mortgage loan structuring, one of the most powerful applications is not just helping borrowers purchase property—but helping them unlock the equity they already have. Cash-out refinancing, equity extraction, and liquidity engineering are where bank statement loans become true wealth-building tools. This chapter focuses on how to strategically access equity, structure cash-out transactions, and position borrowers to use their capital effectively without relying on traditional income documentation.

Most borrowers view their home or investment property as a static asset. They build equity over time through appreciation and loan paydown, but they often do not understand how to access that equity in a strategic way. Advanced professionals recognize that equity is not just value—it is opportunity. When structured correctly, it can be converted into liquidity that can be used to pay off debt, invest in additional properties, or strengthen financial stability. Cash-out refinancing is one of the primary tools for accessing equity. In a typical scenario, the borrower replaces their existing mortgage with a new loan that is larger than the current balance, receiving the difference as cash. For self-employed borrowers who cannot qualify using tax returns, bank statement loans provide a flexible pathway to achieve this.

The first step in structuring a cash-out transaction is understanding the borrower's current equity position. This involves determining the property value, the existing loan balance, and the maximum allowable loan-to-value ratio. Most lenders limit cash-out transactions to a specific LTV, often ranging from 70% to 80% depending on the borrower profile and property type.

Once the maximum loan amount is established, the next step is income qualification. This is where advanced bank statement analysis comes into play. By optimizing income through deposit analysis and expense ratio strategies, you can increase the borrower's qualifying income and support a larger loan amount.

Another important consideration is the purpose of the cash-out. Lenders may evaluate how the borrower intends to use the funds, especially for larger transactions. Common uses include debt consolidation, home improvements, business investment, or purchasing additional real estate. Clearly documenting and explaining the purpose can strengthen the file and improve approval odds.

Debt consolidation is one of the most common and effective uses of cash-out refinancing. By using equity to pay off high-interest debt, borrowers can reduce their monthly obligations and improve their overall financial position. This can also improve their debt-to-income ratio, making it easier to qualify for the new loan.

Liquidity engineering goes beyond simple cash-out transactions. It involves strategically managing a borrower's assets, income, and debt to create financial flexibility. This might include structuring loans to maximize available cash, timing refinances to align with market conditions, or combining multiple strategies to achieve specific goals.

Another advanced concept is maintaining reserves after a cash-out transaction. While it may be tempting for borrowers to use all available funds, lenders typically require a certain level of reserves to ensure financial stability. Advanced structuring involves balancing the amount of cash taken out with the need to maintain sufficient reserves.

Interest rate considerations are also important in cash-out transactions. In some cases, the new loan may have a higher interest rate than the existing loan. Advanced professionals help borrowers evaluate whether the benefits of accessing equity outweigh the potential increase in cost. This involves analyzing the overall financial impact, including monthly payments and long-term goals.

Another key factor is property type. Cash-out guidelines can vary depending on whether the property is a primary residence, second home, or investment property. Investment properties often have stricter LTV limits and higher reserve requirements. Understanding these differences allows you to structure the transaction appropriately.

Timing plays a critical role in equity extraction. Property values, interest rates, and borrower income can all change over time. Advanced professionals evaluate whether it is the right time to refinance or whether waiting could result in a better outcome. For example, waiting for property appreciation or improved income can increase the available cash-out amount.

Another strategy involves using cash-out funds to acquire additional properties. This creates a cycle of leverage, where equity from one property is used to acquire another, which in turn generates income and builds additional equity. This approach is commonly used by real estate investors to scale their portfolios. Risk management is essential in these scenarios. While leveraging equity can accelerate growth, it also increases exposure. Advanced structuring involves ensuring that the borrower can comfortably manage the new loan and that the overall financial structure remains sustainable.

Documentation remains a key component of cash-out transactions. In addition to bank statements and income analysis, lenders may require appraisals, payoff statements, and documentation of how funds will be used. Ensuring that all documentation is complete and consistent is critical for a smooth approval process.

Communication with the borrower is also important. Many borrowers are unfamiliar with the details of cash-out refinancing and may have concerns about increasing their loan balance. By clearly explaining the benefits, risks, and long-term strategy, you can help them make informed decisions.

Another advanced concept is structuring multiple transactions over time. Instead of a single large cash-out, borrowers may benefit from a series of smaller, strategically timed refinances. This allows them to adapt to changing conditions and optimize their financial position.

As you develop your expertise in cash-out strategies and

liquidity engineering, you will begin to see opportunities that go beyond traditional lending. You will be able to help borrowers unlock value, create flexibility, and achieve their financial goals in ways they may not have considered.

Ultimately, this chapter highlights the transformative potential of bank statement loans. They are not just a tool for qualification—they are a gateway to financial strategy and growth. By mastering these techniques, you position yourself as a high-level advisor capable of delivering meaningful results.

Real-Life Math Example: Structuring a Cash-Out Refinance to Build Liquidity and Acquire Additional Assets

Consider a self-employed borrower who owns a primary residence valued at $1,000,000 with an existing mortgage balance of $500,000. This means the borrower has $500,000 in equity. The borrower wants to access this equity to pay off debt and invest in an additional property.

The lender allows a maximum loan-to-value ratio of 75% for cash-out refinancing. This means the maximum loan amount is $750,000. After paying off the existing mortgage of $500,000, the borrower can receive up to $250,000 in cash.

Next, the borrower's income is analyzed using bank statements. The borrower provides 12 months of statements showing average monthly deposits of $30,000. After applying a 40% expense ratio, the qualifying income is $18,000 per month. The borrower has existing debts of $3,000 per month. With a maximum DTI of 50%, the borrower can allocate up to $9,000 toward housing expenses. After subtracting existing debts, the borrower has $6,000 available for the new mortgage payment.

At an interest rate of 7%, a $6,000 monthly payment supports a loan amount of approximately $900,000. Since the required loan amount for the cash-out refinance is $750,000, the borrower qualifies comfortably based on income.

Now consider how the cash-out funds are used. The borrower allocates $100,000 to pay off high-interest credit card and personal loan debt, reducing their monthly obligations by $2,000. This improves their financial position and increases available cash flow.

The remaining $150,000 is used as a down payment on an investment property valued at $600,000. This property generates rental income of $3,000 per month. After expenses, the net income is approximately $2,000 per month.

Now consider the combined impact. The borrower's monthly debt has been reduced by $2,000, and they have added

$2,000 in net rental income. This results in a net improvement of $4,000 per month in cash flow.

Additionally, the borrower now owns two properties with a combined value of $1.6 million. As these properties appreciate and the loans are paid down, the borrower's equity continues to grow.

Over time, the borrower may repeat this process, using equity from one property to acquire another. This creates a cycle of growth and wealth building.

Without advanced structuring, the borrower might not have been able to access this equity or use it effectively. By optimizing income, selecting the right lender, and structuring the transaction strategically, the loan professional enables the borrower to achieve their goals.

This example demonstrates the power of cash-out strategies and liquidity engineering. It shows how bank statement loans can be used not just for qualification, but as a tool for financial growth and opportunity.

As you apply these strategies, you will gain the ability to help borrowers unlock their potential and create long-term value through smart financing decisions.

Chapter 9

Advanced Deal Structuring for Complex Borrowers and Edge Scenarios

At the highest level of bank statement mortgage loan structuring, you are no longer working with straightforward files. You are dealing with complex borrowers, layered income streams, imperfect credit histories, multiple properties, and scenarios that fall outside standard guidelines. This is where true expertise is developed. Advanced deal structuring is the ability to take these edge cases and transform them into approved, well-structured loans by combining everything you have learned—income engineering, risk layering, lender selection, documentation, and timing—into one cohesive strategy.

Complex borrowers often do not fit neatly into predefined categories. They may have multiple businesses, inconsistent income streams, recent credit events, or a mix of personal and business finances that are intertwined. The key is not to force these borrowers into a rigid framework, but to build a custom structure that aligns with their unique situation while still meeting lender guidelines. One of the most common complex scenarios involves borrowers with multiple income streams. For example, a borrower may operate a primary business, own rental properties, and generate additional income from side ventures. Each of these income sources must be analyzed separately and then combined strategically. Advanced structuring involves determining which income sources are strongest, which are most stable, and how they can be layered together to create a comprehensive income profile.

Another challenging scenario is borrowers with recent credit events, such as late payments, collections, or even prior bankruptcies or foreclosures. While these issues can create obstacles, they do not automatically disqualify the borrower. Advanced structuring involves identifying lenders with more flexible seasoning requirements and layering compensating factors such as strong income, low loan-to-value ratios, and significant reserves to offset the risk.

Borrowers with high debt levels also present unique challenges. In these cases, managing debt-to-income ratio becomes critical. This may involve paying off certain debts, restructuring obligations, or selecting loan programs that allow for higher DTIs. Advanced professionals evaluate each debt individually to determine its impact and identify opportunities to improve the overall ratio.

Another complex scenario involves borrowers with mixed-use finances, where personal and business funds are commingled.

This can make deposit analysis more difficult and raise concerns during underwriting. Advanced structuring requires isolating qualifying income, documenting the flow of funds, and presenting a clear explanation of how the borrower's finances operate. This often involves detailed deposit summaries and narrative explanations.

Foreign national borrowers or borrowers with unique residency statuses can also fall into this category. These borrowers may have income generated outside the United States or limited domestic credit history. Advanced structuring involves identifying lenders that specialize in these scenarios and understanding the specific documentation requirements. This may include alternative forms of credit verification, international bank statements, or additional reserves.

Another important category of complex borrowers includes real estate investors with multiple properties. These borrowers often have layered income streams, varying property performance, and higher overall debt levels. Advanced structuring involves analyzing each property's contribution to the borrower's income, evaluating overall portfolio performance, and presenting a consolidated financial picture that demonstrates stability and profitability. Short-term rental properties, such as those used for platforms like Airbnb, introduce additional complexity. Income from these properties can be variable and may require specialized analysis. Advanced professionals understand how to document this income, whether through bank statements, rental histories, or third-party data, and how to present it in a way that aligns with lender guidelines.

Another advanced scenario involves borrowers who are close to qualifying but fall just short in one area. These "near-miss" files require creative structuring. This might involve adjusting the loan amount, increasing the down payment, selecting a different lender, or combining multiple compensating factors. The ability to identify and execute these adjustments is a key skill at this level.

Business owners with multiple entities present another layer of complexity. Income may be distributed across several accounts and entities, making it more challenging to calculate and document. Advanced structuring involves consolidating this information, identifying the primary sources of income, and presenting a unified financial profile.

Another important concept is scenario modeling. Before submitting a loan, advanced professionals often run multiple scenarios to determine the best possible structure. This might include comparing different lenders, adjusting expense ratios, or testing various loan amounts. By evaluating these options in advance, you can select the strategy that provides the highest likelihood of approval.

Risk tolerance varies significantly between lenders, and understanding these differences is essential when working with complex borrowers. Some lenders are more willing to approve loans with layered risk, while others require more conservative profiles. Matching the borrower to the right lender is often the key to success in these scenarios.

Documentation becomes even more critical in complex deals. The more complex the borrower's situation, the more important it is to provide clear, detailed, and well-organized documentation. This includes not only financial documents but also written explanations that guide the underwriter through the file.

Communication is also essential. Complex deals often require more interaction with the lender, including pre-submission discussions, clarification of guidelines, and ongoing communication during underwriting. Building strong relationships with lenders can make a significant difference in these situations.

Another advanced strategy is restructuring the borrower's financial behavior before applying. This might include separating personal and business accounts, stabilizing income patterns, or improving credit. While this requires time and planning, it can significantly improve the outcome of the loan.

Flexibility and adaptability are key traits when working with complex borrowers. Each scenario is unique, and there is rarely a single correct approach. Advanced professionals remain open to multiple solutions and adjust their strategies based on the specific circumstances.

Ultimately, advanced deal structuring is about problem-solving. It is about taking complex, imperfect situations and finding a path to approval. This requires a deep understanding of guidelines, a strategic mindset, and the ability to think creatively while staying within the boundaries of compliance.

As you master these skills, you will be able to handle increasingly complex scenarios with confidence. You will become the professional who can close deals that others cannot, providing value to both borrowers and lenders. This is the highest level of bank statement mortgage loan structuring.

Real-Life Math Example: Structuring a Complex Multi-Income Borrower for Approval

Consider a self-employed borrower who owns two businesses, has rental income from two properties, and is applying for a bank statement mortgage loan to purchase a new primary residence. The borrower provides 12 months of bank statements for both businesses, as well as documentation for rental income.

The first business shows total deposits of $240,000 over 12 months, averaging $20,000 per month. After excluding $20,000 in non-recurring deposits, the adjusted total is $220,000, resulting in an average monthly deposit of approximately $18,333. Applying a 40% expense ratio, the qualifying income from this business is approximately $11,000 per month.

The second business shows total deposits of $120,000 over 12 months, averaging $10,000 per month. After excluding $10,000 in transfers, the adjusted total is $110,000, resulting in an average monthly deposit of approximately $9,167. Applying a 30% expense ratio, the qualifying income from this business is approximately $6,417 per month.

The borrower also has two rental properties generating net income of $1,500 per month each, for a total of $3,000 in additional income. When combined, the borrower's total qualifying income is approximately $20,417 per month.

The borrower has existing debts totaling $4,000 per month. Using a maximum DTI of 50%, the borrower can allocate up to $10,208 toward housing expenses. After subtracting existing debts, the borrower has approximately $6,208 available for a mortgage payment.

At an interest rate of 7%, this supports a loan amount of approximately $950,000. However, the borrower has a credit score of 655 and limited reserves of $60,000, which may raise concerns for the lender.

To address these issues, the borrower increases the down payment, reducing the loan amount and improving the LTV. The borrower also provides additional documentation showing consistent business growth and stable rental income, which helps offset the lower credit score.

Additionally, the loan professional selects a lender that allows higher DTIs and is more flexible with credit requirements. This alignment improves the likelihood of approval.

Now consider an alternative scenario where the loan professional only used one business's income and ignored the second business and rental income. The qualifying income would be significantly lower, resulting in a reduced loan amount or potential denial. By layering multiple income sources, the borrower is able to qualify for a much higher loan.

This example demonstrates the importance of analyzing all available income sources and combining them strategically. It also highlights the need to address weaknesses such as credit and reserves through compensating factors and lender selection.

Through advanced structuring, the borrower's complex financial profile is transformed into a clear and approvable loan file. This is the essence of working with complex borrowers—identifying opportunities, addressing challenges, and creating a structured path to approval.

As you continue to apply these principles, you will develop the ability to handle even the most challenging scenarios and achieve consistent success in bank statement mortgage loan structuring.

Chapter 10

Building a Repeatable System for High-Level Bank Statement Loan Approvals

At the highest level of bank statement mortgage loan structuring, success is no longer based on individual deals—it is based on systems. While the previous chapters have focused on specific strategies such as income engineering, risk layering, lender selection, documentation, and timing, this chapter brings everything together into a repeatable, scalable process. The goal is to create a system that allows you to consistently analyze, structure, and close complex bank statement loans with precision and confidence.

Most loan professionals operate on a deal-by-deal basis, reacting to each borrower's situation as it arises. While this approach can work, it often leads to inconsistency and inefficiency. Advanced professionals, on the other hand, develop structured workflows that guide them through each stage of the loan process. This allows them to handle a higher volume of deals while maintaining a high level of quality and accuracy.

The first component of a repeatable system is intake analysis. This is where you gather all relevant information about the borrower, including income sources, bank statements, credit profile, debts, reserves, and property details. The goal is to create a complete picture of the borrower's financial situation before making any decisions. Advanced professionals use standardized checklists to ensure that no critical information is overlooked.

Once the initial data is collected, the next step is income engineering. This involves analyzing deposits, identifying qualifying income, applying appropriate expense ratios, and determining the most effective way to present income. At this stage, you should also evaluate whether additional documentation, such as a CPA-prepared profit and loss statement, could improve the outcome.

The third step is risk assessment. This involves evaluating the borrower's credit, debt-to-income ratio, loan-to-value ratio, reserves, and overall risk profile. The goal is to identify both strengths and weaknesses within the file. Advanced structuring involves not only identifying these factors but also determining how they interact and how they can be balanced.

The fourth step is scenario modeling. Before selecting a lender or submitting the loan, advanced professionals run multiple scenarios to determine the best possible structure. This might include testing different expense ratios, adjusting loan amounts, or comparing lender guidelines. By evaluating these options in advance, you can select the strategy that provides the highest likelihood of approval.

Lender selection is the next critical step. Based on the borrower's profile and the results of your scenario modeling, you choose the lender whose guidelines best align with the file. This step requires a deep understanding of investor overlays and program variations. Advanced professionals maintain a network of lenders and stay updated on their guidelines to ensure optimal matching.

Once the lender is selected, the next step is documentation preparation. This involves organizing all required documents, creating income worksheets, preparing loan summaries, and ensuring that all information is consistent and complete. A well-prepared file reduces the likelihood of conditions and speeds up the underwriting process.

Submission strategy is another important component of the system. This includes deciding when to submit the loan, ensuring that all variables are optimized, and presenting the file in a way that highlights its strengths. Advanced professionals avoid rushed submissions and prioritize quality over speed.

The underwriting phase is where your preparation is tested. During this stage, clear communication and responsiveness are essential. Addressing conditions quickly and providing additional documentation when needed helps keep the process moving smoothly. Advanced professionals anticipate potential conditions and address them proactively.

Another key component of a repeatable system is post-closing analysis. After each loan closes, you should review the file to identify what worked well and what could be improved. This continuous feedback loop allows you to refine your process and improve future outcomes.

Automation can also play a role in building a scalable system. Tools such as spreadsheets, templates, and CRM systems can help streamline repetitive tasks and ensure consistency. For example, standardized income calculation templates can reduce errors and improve efficiency.

Another important aspect is borrower education. By educating borrowers on how their financial behavior impacts the loan process, you can improve the quality of the files you receive. This might include guidance on maintaining clean bank statements, avoiding large unexplained deposits, and managing credit effectively.

Team structure is also relevant for those looking to scale. As your volume increases, delegating certain tasks such as document collection or initial analysis can allow you to focus on high-level structuring and strategy. Building a team with clear roles and responsibilities can significantly improve efficiency.

Consistency is the foundation of any successful system. By following a structured process for each loan, you reduce variability and increase the likelihood of consistent outcomes. This also allows you to handle more complex files with confidence, as you have a proven framework to guide your decisions.

Another advanced concept is building relationships with lenders and underwriters. Strong relationships can lead to better communication, faster approvals, and greater flexibility in complex scenarios. Over time, these relationships become a valuable asset that enhances your ability to close deals.

As you refine your system, you will begin to develop intuition. You will be able to quickly identify the strengths and weaknesses of a file, anticipate potential issues, and determine the best course of action. This level of expertise comes from experience and repetition, reinforced by a structured approach.

Ultimately, building a repeatable system transforms your approach from reactive to proactive. Instead of solving problems as they arise, you anticipate and prevent them. Instead of relying on luck, you rely on process. This shift not only improves your results but also reduces stress and increases efficiency.

This chapter represents the culmination of the entire series. By integrating all the concepts you have learned into a cohesive system, you gain the ability to consistently structure and close high-level bank statement mortgage loans. This is what separates top performers in the industry from the rest.

Real-Life Math Example: Applying a Repeatable System to Structure a High-Level Loan

Consider a self-employed borrower who owns an e-commerce business and is applying for a bank statement mortgage loan to purchase a primary residence. The borrower provides 12 months of business bank statements showing total deposits of $480,000, averaging $40,000 per month.

During the intake analysis, it is identified that $60,000 of the deposits are non-recurring transfers and refunds. After excluding these deposits, the adjusted total is $420,000, resulting in an average monthly deposit of $35,000.

In the income engineering phase, a standard expense ratio of 50% would result in a qualifying income of $17,500 per month. However, the borrower provides a CPA-prepared profit and loss statement showing actual expenses of 30%. Applying this lower expense ratio increases the qualifying income to $24,500 per month.

Next, the risk assessment reveals that the borrower has a credit score of 690, existing debts of $3,000 per month, and $150,000 in reserves. Using a maximum DTI of 50%, the borrower can allocate up to $12,250 toward housing expenses. After subtracting existing debts, the borrower has $9,250 available for a mortgage payment.

At an interest rate of 7%, this supports a loan amount of approximately $1.4 million. However, scenario modeling reveals that by slightly reducing the loan amount and increasing the down payment, the borrower can achieve a lower LTV and better pricing.

The lender selection process identifies a lender that allows a 30% expense ratio and offers competitive terms for borrowers with strong reserves. This alignment ensures that the borrower's income is maximized while meeting lender guidelines.

During documentation preparation, the loan professional creates a detailed income worksheet, organizes all bank statements, and prepares a loan summary that explains the borrower's business and income calculation. This ensures that the file is clear and easy to review.

The loan is submitted at a time when the borrower's bank statements reflect strong and consistent income, and all variables are optimized. During underwriting, conditions are minimal due to the thorough preparation.

After closing, the loan professional reviews the file and identifies key factors that contributed to the successful outcome, such as the use of a CPA-prepared P&L, strong reserves, and strategic lender selection. These insights are incorporated into the system for future use.

Now consider if this loan had been approached without a structured system. The loan professional might have applied a standard 50% expense ratio, resulting in a qualifying income of $17,500 per month. This would have reduced the maximum loan amount significantly, potentially limiting the borrower's options or leading to a denial.

By following a repeatable system, the loan professional was able to optimize each component of the file and achieve a significantly better outcome. This demonstrates the power of a structured approach and the importance of integrating all aspects of advanced bank statement mortgage loan structuring.

As you apply this system to your own work, you will develop the ability to consistently deliver high-level results, handle complex scenarios, and build a successful and scalable mortgage business.

Chapter 11

Scaling Volume, Building Pipelines, and Turning Expertise into Consistent Income

At this stage of your journey through advanced bank statement mortgage loan structuring, you have developed the technical ability to analyze complex files, engineer income, layer risk, select the right lenders, and present strong, approvable loan packages. However, mastery is not only about structuring individual deals—it is about scaling your ability to consistently generate, manage, and close a high volume of profitable loans. This chapter focuses on how to turn your expertise into a predictable system for income, growth, and long-term success.

Scaling begins with understanding that deal flow is the lifeblood of your business. Even the most skilled loan professional cannot succeed without a steady pipeline of opportunities. Advanced professionals do not rely on random referrals or inconsistent marketing—they build intentional systems to attract, qualify, and convert borrowers who are ideal candidates for bank statement loans.

One of the most powerful strategies for building pipeline is niche positioning. Instead of trying to serve every borrower, you focus on a specific segment of the market—self-employed individuals, business owners, real estate investors, 1099 earners, or high-income professionals who cannot qualify through traditional documentation. By specializing in this niche, you become known as the expert who solves complex income problems. This positioning not only attracts more qualified leads but also reduces competition.

Marketing for bank statement loans is fundamentally different from traditional mortgage marketing. Your messaging must speak directly to the pain points of your target audience. Many self-employed borrowers have been denied loans due to tax write-offs or inconsistent income. Your marketing should clearly communicate that you understand their situation and offer a solution. This includes using language such as "qualify without tax returns," "use bank statements instead of W-2s," and "get approved as a business owner."

Lead generation channels can include digital advertising, social media, email campaigns, partnerships with real estate agents, and referral networks. Each channel should be designed to attract borrowers who fit your niche. Advanced professionals often use targeted ads that highlight specific scenarios, such as "self-employed and denied for a mortgage?" or "1099 income? You may still qualify." Once leads are generated, the next step is qualification. Not every lead will be a good fit for a bank statement loan, and it is important to identify strong candidates early in the process. This involves gathering key information such as income sources, bank statements, credit profile, and loan goals. By quickly identifying viable borrowers, you can focus your time and energy on deals that are more likely to close.

The conversion process is where your structuring expertise becomes a competitive advantage. Many borrowers have been told "no" by other lenders. When you can confidently analyze their situation, explain how they can qualify, and present a clear path forward, you build trust and increase the likelihood of conversion. This is where education and communication play a critical role.

Another important aspect of scaling is time management. As your volume increases, you must prioritize high-value activities and streamline repetitive tasks. This might include using templates for income calculations, automating parts of the document collection process, or delegating administrative tasks. The goal is to focus your time on structuring deals and building relationships rather than getting bogged down in manual processes.

Building a team is often necessary for scaling. This may include loan processors, assistants, or junior loan officers who can handle specific parts of the workflow. By delegating tasks such as document collection, file organization, and initial analysis, you can increase your capacity and handle more deals simultaneously.

Another key component is pipeline management. Advanced professionals track their deals at every stage, from initial inquiry to closing. This allows them to identify bottlenecks, prioritize follow-ups, and ensure that no opportunities are lost. A well-managed pipeline provides visibility into your business and helps you maintain consistent production.

Follow-up is critical in converting leads into closed deals. Many borrowers are not ready to move forward immediately, but may become viable candidates over time. By maintaining regular communication and providing value, you can stay top of mind and convert these leads when they are ready.

Another advanced strategy is creating multiple entry points into your business. This might include offering free consultations, educational content, or tools such as income calculators or loan qualification guides. These entry points attract potential borrowers and allow you to demonstrate your expertise before asking for a commitment.

Partnerships can also play a significant role in scaling. Real estate agents, financial advisors, accountants, and business consultants often work with the same type of clients who need bank statement loans. By building relationships with these professionals, you can create a steady stream of referrals.

Another important concept is repeat business. Many borrowers, especially real estate investors and business owners, will need financing multiple times over the course of their careers. By providing a strong experience and maintaining relationships, you can generate repeat transactions and build a loyal client base.

Revenue optimization is also part of scaling. This involves structuring deals in a way that maximizes both borrower benefit and business profitability. This might include offering different loan options, adjusting loan amounts, or focusing on higher-value transactions.

Tracking performance is essential for continuous improvement. By analyzing metrics such as conversion rates, average loan size, and time to close, you can identify areas for improvement and refine your strategies. This data-driven approach allows you to scale more effectively.

Another advanced concept is leveraging your expertise to create additional income streams. This might include teaching others, creating courses, or offering consulting services. By sharing your knowledge, you not only generate additional revenue but also establish yourself as a leader in the industry.

Mindset is also a critical factor in scaling. Moving from a deal-by-deal approach to a system-driven business requires discipline, consistency, and a long-term perspective. Advanced professionals focus on building sustainable systems rather than chasing short-term wins.

Ultimately, scaling your business is about leverage. It is about using your knowledge, systems, and relationships to create consistent and predictable results. When done correctly, it allows you to handle more deals, serve more clients, and generate higher income without increasing stress.

This chapter represents the transition from technician to business builder. By applying these principles, you can turn your expertise in bank statement mortgage loan structuring into a scalable and highly profitable business.

Real-Life Math Example: Scaling Monthly Production and Income Using a Structured Pipeline

Consider a loan professional who specializes in bank statement mortgage loans and wants to scale their business. Initially, they are closing 3 loans per month, with an average loan amount of $600,000 and an average commission of 1%. This results in monthly revenue of $18,000. To scale, the loan professional focuses on increasing lead generation, improving conversion rates, and optimizing deal size. They implement a targeted marketing campaign that generates 60 leads per month. After initial qualification, 30 of these leads are identified as viable candidates.

From these 30 qualified leads, the loan professional converts 10 into active applications. With a closing rate of 60%, this results in 6 closed loans per month—doubling their original production.

Next, the loan professional focuses on increasing the average loan size through advanced structuring. By optimizing income calculations, selecting better lenders, and improving borrower positioning, they increase the average loan amount from $600,000 to $800,000.

With 6 loans per month at an average of $800,000 and a 1% commission, monthly revenue increases to $48,000. This represents a significant improvement from the original $18,000.

Now consider the impact of improving conversion rates. By refining their sales process and improving communication, the loan professional increases their conversion rate from 33% (10 out of 30) to 50% (15 out of 30). With the same 60% closing rate, this results in 9 closed loans per month. At 9 loans per month with an average loan amount of $800,000, total monthly volume reaches $7.2 million. At a 1% commission, this results in monthly revenue of $72,000.

Next, the loan professional builds a small team, including a processor and an assistant, allowing them to handle more volume without increasing their workload significantly. With improved efficiency, they increase their closing capacity to 12 loans per month.

At 12 loans per month with an average loan amount of $800,000, total monthly volume reaches $9.6 million. At a 1% commission, monthly revenue increases to $96,000.

Now consider the annual impact. At $96,000 per month, the loan professional generates over $1.15 million in annual revenue. This demonstrates the power of scaling through systems, pipeline management, and advanced structuring.

Additionally, by building relationships and generating repeat business, the loan professional reduces reliance on new lead generation, further stabilizing their pipeline.

This example illustrates how scaling is not just about working harder—it is about working smarter. By increasing lead flow, improving conversion rates, optimizing loan size, and building systems, you can significantly increase your production and income. As you apply these principles, you will begin to see your business transform from a series of individual deals into a scalable, system-driven operation capable of producing consistent and high-level results.

Chapter 12

Mastery, Long-Term Strategy, and Becoming the Go-To Authority in Bank Statement Lending

Reaching the highest level of bank statement mortgage loan structuring is not just about closing more deals—it is about becoming the professional that others rely on when deals are complex, when borrowers have been turned down elsewhere, and when creative solutions are required. Mastery is the ability to consistently produce results across different market conditions, borrower profiles, and lender environments. It is also about building a long-term strategy that turns your expertise into a durable, scalable, and respected business.

At this level, your focus shifts from individual transactions to long-term positioning. You are no longer just solving problems—you are anticipating them. You begin to see patterns in borrower behavior, lender guidelines, and market trends. This awareness allows you to stay ahead of changes and adapt your strategies proactively rather than reactively.

One of the key elements of mastery is consistency. Anyone can close a complex deal occasionally, but true expertise is demonstrated by the ability to do it repeatedly. This requires discipline, attention to detail, and a commitment to following the systems you have built. Every file is approached with the same level of care, regardless of size or complexity.

Another critical component is specialization. While it may be tempting to handle all types of loans, focusing on bank statement loans allows you to develop deep expertise and stand out in the market. By positioning yourself as a specialist, you attract borrowers and referral partners who specifically need your skills. This not only increases your deal flow but also improves the quality of your pipeline.

Authority is built through visibility and value. This means consistently sharing your knowledge, whether through content, consultations, or partnerships. When you educate borrowers and industry professionals about bank statement loans, you position yourself as the expert who understands and solves these challenges. Over time, this builds trust and credibility.

Content creation is one of the most effective ways to establish authority. This can include videos, articles, social media posts, or even educational courses. The goal is to address common questions and challenges faced by your target audience. For example, explaining how self-employed borrowers can qualify without tax returns or how to structure income using bank statements can attract highly qualified leads. Another important aspect of long-term strategy is relationship building. Strong relationships with real estate agents, accountants, financial advisors, and other professionals can provide a steady stream of referrals. These partners often encounter clients who need specialized financing solutions, and by positioning yourself as the expert, you become their go-to resource.

Client relationships are equally important. Providing a high level of service and maintaining communication even after the loan closes can lead to repeat business and referrals. Many self-employed borrowers will need financing multiple times, whether for refinancing, purchasing additional properties, or expanding their investments.

Market awareness is another key element of mastery. Interest rates, lender guidelines, and economic conditions are constantly changing. Staying informed allows you to adjust your strategies and provide relevant advice to your clients. For example, during periods of rising interest rates, borrowers may need to focus more on improving income or reducing debt to qualify.

Another advanced concept is portfolio thinking. Instead of viewing each loan as a standalone transaction, you begin to think in terms of the borrower's long-term financial goals. This might involve helping an investor build a portfolio of properties or guiding a business owner through multiple financing strategies over time. By taking a long-term approach, you create more opportunities and provide greater value.

Efficiency and scalability remain important at this level. As your business grows, maintaining quality while increasing volume requires strong systems and processes. This includes refining your workflows, leveraging technology, and building a team that supports your operations.

Another key aspect of mastery is adaptability. No two deals are exactly the same, and the ability to adjust your approach based on the specific circumstances is critical. This requires a deep understanding of guidelines, as well as the creativity to find solutions within those boundaries.

Risk management also evolves at this level. You are not only evaluating risk for individual deals but also for your overall business. This includes managing pipeline quality, ensuring compliance, and maintaining strong relationships with lenders. By managing risk effectively, you create a stable and sustainable business.

Mentorship and teaching are often natural extensions of mastery. As you gain experience, you may find opportunities to train others, whether within your organization or through external platforms. Teaching not only reinforces your own knowledge but also expands your influence and impact.

Another important element is reputation. In the mortgage industry, reputation is everything. Being known as someone who can close complex deals, communicate effectively, and deliver results consistently will set you apart. This reputation becomes a powerful asset that attracts opportunities and builds trust.

Financial management is also part of long-term success. As your income grows, managing expenses, reinvesting in your business, and planning for the future become increasingly important. This ensures that your success is not only achieved but sustained.

Mindset plays a crucial role in reaching and maintaining mastery. This includes staying focused, continuously learning, and maintaining a high level of professionalism. Challenges and setbacks are inevitable, but how you respond to them determines your long-term success.

Ultimately, becoming the go-to authority in bank statement lending is about combining expertise, systems, relationships, and strategy. It is about consistently delivering value, adapting to change, and building a business that stands the test of time. This chapter represents the culmination of the entire series. By applying these principles, you can move beyond individual deals and build a lasting presence in the mortgage industry. You become not just a loan professional, but a trusted advisor and expert in your field.

Real-Life Math Example: Building Long-Term Wealth Through Strategic Loan Structuring

Consider a self-employed borrower who owns a consulting business and is looking to build a real estate portfolio over time. The borrower starts with 12 months of bank statements showing total deposits of $360,000, averaging $30,000 per month. After applying a 40% expense ratio, the qualifying income is $18,000 per month.

With existing debts of $3,000 per month and a maximum DTI of 50%, the borrower can allocate up to $9,000 toward housing expenses. After subtracting existing debts, the borrower has $6,000 available for a mortgage payment. At an interest rate of 7%, this supports a loan amount of approximately $900,000.

The borrower purchases a primary residence using this loan. Over time, the borrower's income increases, and they accumulate additional reserves. After one year, the borrower provides updated bank statements showing average monthly deposits of $40,000. Applying the same expense ratio, the qualifying income increases to $24,000 per month. With improved income and additional reserves, the borrower now qualifies for a second loan to purchase an investment property. The rental income from this property adds an additional $2,500 per month to the borrower's income, further strengthening their profile.

Over the next few years, the borrower continues to acquire properties, each time using advanced structuring to maximize qualifying income and manage risk. By the fifth year, the borrower owns four properties, each generating rental income and contributing to overall financial growth.

Now consider the cumulative impact. The borrower's total monthly income, including business and rental income, reaches $35,000. With strategic structuring, the borrower is able to continue qualifying for additional loans while maintaining a manageable risk profile.

Assuming an average property value of $800,000 and an annual appreciation rate of 5%, the borrower's portfolio grows significantly in value over time. After five years, the total portfolio value exceeds $4 million, with substantial equity built through both appreciation and loan amortization.

This example demonstrates how advanced bank statement loan structuring can be used not only to secure individual loans but also to build long-term wealth. By strategically managing income, leveraging financing options, and planning for the future, borrowers can achieve significant financial growth.

For the loan professional, this represents an opportunity to build long-term relationships and generate repeat business. Each transaction builds on the previous one, creating a cycle of growth and opportunity.

This is the ultimate goal of mastery—not just closing deals, but creating lasting impact and value for both yourself and your clients.

Chapter 13

Legacy-Level Structuring, Wealth Engineering, and Creating Generational Impact Through Bank Statement Lending

At the highest level of mastery, bank statement mortgage loan structuring evolves beyond transactions, pipelines, and even business growth. It becomes a vehicle for wealth engineering—both for your clients and for yourself. This chapter focuses on how to use everything you have learned to help borrowers build long-term wealth, create generational assets, and position themselves for financial independence. At the same time, it shows how you, as a professional, can leverage your expertise to build a legacy-level business that compounds over time.

Most borrowers initially approach financing with a short-term mindset. They want to buy a home, refinance a property, or access equity. While these are valid goals, advanced professionals recognize that each loan is part of a larger financial strategy. Instead of asking, "How do we get this deal approved?" you begin asking, "How does this loan fit into the borrower's long-term wealth plan?" This shift in thinking is what separates transactional professionals from strategic advisors. You are no longer just facilitating loans—you are helping design financial pathways that can impact a borrower's life for decades. Bank statement loans, with their flexibility and adaptability, are uniquely positioned to support this type of strategy, especially for self-employed individuals and investors.

One of the core principles of wealth engineering is leverage. Real estate financing allows borrowers to control large assets with relatively small amounts of capital. By strategically structuring loans, borrowers can acquire properties, generate income, and benefit from appreciation over time. Advanced structuring ensures that each loan is optimized not only for approval but also for long-term sustainability.

Another key concept is cash flow optimization. It is not enough for a borrower to qualify for a loan—they must also be able to manage it comfortably. This involves structuring payments, selecting appropriate loan terms, and ensuring that the property generates sufficient income. For investors, this means analyzing rental income, expenses, and market conditions to create positive or at least stable cash flow.

Equity growth is another critical component of long-term strategy. As borrowers make payments and property values increase, they build equity that can be leveraged for future investments. Advanced professionals help borrowers understand how to access this equity through refinancing or home equity strategies, creating a cycle of growth and reinvestment.

Portfolio building is where these concepts come together. Instead of focusing on a single property, borrowers begin to acquire multiple properties over time, each contributing to overall income and net worth. Advanced structuring allows borrowers to qualify for additional loans by optimizing income, managing debt, and selecting the right programs.

Risk management becomes even more important at this level. As borrowers take on more properties and larger loan amounts, the potential impact of market changes or income fluctuations increases. Advanced structuring involves creating buffers, such as reserves, diversified income streams, and conservative loan structures, to protect against these risks.

Another important aspect is tax efficiency. While bank statement loans do not rely on tax returns for qualification, understanding the tax implications of real estate investments is essential for long-term success. Working with accountants and financial advisors, borrowers can structure their finances in a way that maximizes both loan eligibility and tax benefits.

Business growth is also closely tied to wealth engineering. Many self-employed borrowers experience increasing income over time as their businesses expand. Advanced professionals help these borrowers align their business growth with their financing strategy, ensuring that they can continue to qualify for larger loans and take advantage of new opportunities.

Another advanced concept is exit strategy planning. Every loan and investment should have a long-term plan, whether it is holding the property for income, selling for profit, or refinancing to access equity. By understanding the borrower's goals, you can structure loans that align with these strategies and provide flexibility for future decisions.

For the loan professional, this level of engagement creates deeper relationships and more opportunities. Instead of working with a borrower once, you become their long-term advisor, assisting with multiple transactions over time. This not only increases your income but also builds a strong and loyal client base.

Another key element is scalability. As you help more clients build wealth, your business grows organically through referrals and repeat transactions. This creates a compounding effect, where each successful deal leads to new opportunities.

Technology and systems continue to play a role in supporting this growth. By maintaining organized records, tracking client progress, and managing your pipeline effectively, you can handle a larger volume of high-quality deals without sacrificing service.

Education remains a cornerstone of this process. By teaching borrowers about financing strategies, market trends, and wealth-building principles, you empower them to make informed decisions. This not only improves outcomes but also strengthens your position as a trusted advisor.

Another important aspect is adaptability. Markets change, guidelines evolve, and borrower needs shift over time. Staying informed and adjusting your strategies accordingly ensures that you can continue to provide value in any environment.

Reputation becomes even more valuable at this level. Being known as someone who can help clients build wealth—not just secure loans—sets you apart in the industry. This reputation attracts higher-quality clients and creates long-term opportunities.

Financial discipline is also critical. Both you and your clients must manage resources effectively, avoid over-leveraging, and maintain a long-term perspective. This ensures that growth is sustainable and not driven by short-term gains.

Ultimately, legacy-level structuring is about impact. It is about using your skills to create meaningful and lasting change in the financial lives of your clients. It is about building a business that not only generates income but also contributes to the success of others.

This chapter represents the final evolution of your journey. You are no longer just a loan professional—you are a strategist, an advisor, and a builder of long-term wealth. By applying these principles, you can create a legacy that extends far beyond individual transactions.

Real-Life Math Example: Building a Multi-Property Portfolio and Generational Wealth

Consider a self-employed borrower who owns a digital marketing business and is starting their real estate investment journey. The borrower provides 12 months of bank statements showing total deposits of $480,000, averaging $40,000 per month. After applying a 40% expense ratio, the qualifying income is $24,000 per month.

With existing debts of $4,000 per month and a maximum DTI of 50%, the borrower can allocate up to $12,000 toward housing expenses. After subtracting existing debts, the borrower has $8,000 available for mortgage payments.

At an interest rate of 7%, this supports a loan amount of approximately $1.2 million. The borrower purchases a primary residence for $1 million, using a portion of their available qualification.

After one year, the borrower's business grows, and their average monthly deposits increase to $50,000. Applying the same expense ratio, the qualifying income rises to $30,000 per month. Additionally, the borrower has saved and accumulated $200,000 in reserves.

With improved income and reserves, the borrower qualifies for a second loan to purchase an investment property. The property is purchased for $800,000 and generates rental income of $3,000 per month. This income is added to the borrower's overall profile, further increasing their qualifying capacity.

Over the next three years, the borrower continues to acquire properties using similar strategies. Each property adds rental income, which contributes to the borrower's ability to qualify for additional loans. By the fourth year, the borrower owns four properties with a combined value of $3.5 million.

Assuming an average annual appreciation rate of 5%, the total value of the portfolio grows to approximately $4.25 million. At the same time, the borrower builds equity through loan amortization, increasing their net worth. The borrower also uses refinancing strategies to access equity and reinvest in additional properties. For example, a cash-out refinance on one property may provide funds for a down payment on another, accelerating portfolio growth.

Now consider the long-term impact. Over a 10-year period, the borrower's portfolio could grow to several million dollars in value, with multiple income streams and significant equity. This creates financial stability, passive income, and opportunities for future investments.

For the loan professional, this represents multiple transactions over time, as well as referrals from the borrower to others in similar situations. Each successful deal strengthens the relationship and creates additional opportunities.

This example demonstrates how advanced bank statement loan structuring can be used not just for individual transactions, but as a tool for building long-term wealth. By combining income optimization, strategic financing, and portfolio growth, borrowers can achieve significant financial success.

As you apply these principles, you will move beyond closing loans and into the realm of wealth engineering, creating lasting value for both yourself and your clients.

Chapter 14

Market Cycles, Adaptive Strategies, and Thriving in Any Lending Environment

At the highest level of bank statement mortgage loan structuring, mastery is not only measured by how well you perform in favorable conditions, but by how effectively you adapt when the market shifts. Interest rates rise and fall, lender guidelines tighten and loosen, and borrower behavior evolves based on economic conditions. The professionals who thrive long-term are those who understand market cycles and adjust their strategies accordingly. This chapter focuses on how to remain effective, profitable, and competitive regardless of external conditions.

Every market cycle presents both challenges and opportunities. In a low interest rate environment, demand for mortgage financing tends to increase. Borrowers are more eager to purchase or refinance, and loan volume can grow rapidly. However, competition also increases, and borrowers may have more options. In contrast, rising interest rate environments often reduce overall demand, but they also create opportunities for specialized products like bank statement loans, where borrowers may have fewer alternatives. Understanding these dynamics allows you to position yourself strategically. During periods of high demand, your focus may be on efficiency, scalability, and managing increased volume. During slower periods, your focus shifts to niche targeting, creative structuring, and helping borrowers who may not qualify through traditional methods. Bank statement loans often become more valuable in tighter markets because they provide solutions for borrowers who fall outside standard guidelines.

Interest rates play a central role in shaping borrower behavior. As rates increase, monthly payments rise, which can reduce purchasing power and make qualification more difficult. Advanced professionals anticipate these challenges and adjust their strategies accordingly. This might include structuring smaller loan amounts, increasing down payments, or focusing on borrowers with stronger income profiles.

Another important factor is guideline changes. Lenders continuously adjust their programs based on market conditions and risk tolerance. This may include changes to credit score requirements, debt-to-income limits, loan-to-value ratios, or documentation standards. Staying informed about these changes is essential for maintaining a competitive edge. Advanced professionals regularly review lender updates and adapt their strategies to align with current guidelines. Economic conditions also influence borrower behavior. During periods of economic growth, business owners may experience increased income, making it easier to qualify for loans. During economic downturns, income may become more volatile, requiring more careful analysis and structuring. Understanding these patterns allows you to better assess borrower risk and position files appropriately.

Another key concept is diversification. Relying on a single type of borrower or loan product can make your business vulnerable to market changes. By expanding your expertise across different scenarios—such as primary residences, investment properties, refinancing, and cash-out strategies—you create multiple streams of opportunity. This diversification helps stabilize your business and reduces reliance on any one segment.

Adaptive structuring is a critical skill in changing markets. This involves adjusting your approach based on current conditions. For example, in a rising rate environment, you may focus more on improving borrower qualifications through income optimization or debt reduction. In a declining rate environment, you may focus on refinancing opportunities and maximizing loan amounts.

Another important strategy is focusing on value rather than price. While interest rates are important, borrowers often need guidance and solutions more than the lowest rate. By positioning yourself as an expert who can solve complex problems, you differentiate yourself from competitors who focus solely on pricing.

Communication becomes even more important during market shifts. Borrowers may be uncertain or hesitant, especially during periods of economic change. Providing clear, accurate, and timely information helps build trust and keeps deals moving forward. Advanced professionals take the time to educate borrowers about market conditions and how they impact their options.

Another key element is managing expectations. In changing markets, borrowers may need to adjust their expectations regarding loan amounts, rates, or terms. By setting realistic expectations early in the process, you reduce the likelihood of frustration and improve the overall experience.

Technology and data analysis can also support adaptive strategies. By tracking trends in your pipeline, monitoring conversion rates, and analyzing borrower profiles, you can identify patterns and adjust your approach. This data-driven perspective allows you to make informed decisions and stay ahead of changes.

Another advanced concept is opportunity recognition. Every market cycle creates unique opportunities. For example, rising rates may reduce competition, allowing you to capture a larger share of the market. Economic uncertainty may drive borrowers to seek alternative financing solutions, increasing demand for bank statement loans. By identifying these opportunities, you can position yourself to benefit from changing conditions.

Relationship management becomes even more valuable in uncertain markets. Strong relationships with lenders, referral partners, and clients provide stability and support. These relationships can lead to new opportunities and help you navigate challenges more effectively.

Another important aspect is financial resilience. Managing your own business finances effectively ensures that you can withstand fluctuations in volume and income. This includes maintaining reserves, controlling expenses, and planning for different scenarios.

Mindset is also critical. Market changes can create stress and uncertainty, but they also provide opportunities for growth. Maintaining a positive, proactive mindset allows you to adapt and continue moving forward.

Long-term thinking is essential for sustained success. While short-term fluctuations are inevitable, focusing on long-term goals helps you stay grounded and make strategic decisions. Advanced professionals view market cycles as part of a larger journey rather than isolated events.

Ultimately, thriving in any lending environment requires a combination of knowledge, adaptability, and strategic thinking. By understanding market cycles and adjusting your approach accordingly, you can continue to succeed regardless of external conditions.

This chapter reinforces the idea that mastery is not static—it is dynamic. It evolves with the market and requires continuous learning and adaptation. By embracing this mindset, you position yourself for long-term success in the ever-changing world of mortgage lending.

Real-Life Math Example: Adjusting Loan Strategy in a Rising Interest Rate Environment

Consider a self-employed borrower who is applying for a bank statement mortgage loan during a period of rising interest rates. The borrower provides 12 months of bank statements showing total deposits of $360,000, averaging $30,000 per month. After applying a 40% expense ratio, the qualifying income is $18,000 per month.

The borrower has existing debts of $3,000 per month, and the lender allows a maximum DTI of 50%. This means the borrower can allocate up to $9,000 toward housing expenses. After subtracting existing debts, the borrower has $6,000 available for a mortgage payment. At an interest rate of 5%, this monthly payment would support a loan amount of approximately $1 million. However, due to rising rates, the current interest rate is now 7.5%. At this higher rate, the same $6,000 payment supports a loan amount of approximately $750,000. This represents a significant reduction in purchasing power.

To address this challenge, the loan professional implements several advanced strategies. First, the borrower increases their down payment, reducing the loan amount and improving the loan-to-value ratio. This not only lowers the monthly payment but also strengthens the file.

Next, the borrower focuses on reducing existing debts. By paying off a $1,000 monthly auto loan, the borrower reduces their total debt obligations to $2,000 per month. This increases the amount available for housing expenses to $7,000 per month.

At the same interest rate of 7.5%, a $7,000 monthly payment supports a loan amount of approximately $875,000. This partially offsets the impact of rising rates.

Additionally, the borrower provides a CPA-prepared profit and loss statement that supports a lower expense ratio of 30%. This increases the qualifying income to $21,000 per month. With this higher income, the maximum housing expense at a 50% DTI increases to $10,500. After subtracting existing debts of $2,000, the borrower has $8,500 available for a mortgage payment.

At 7.5%, this supports a loan amount of approximately $1.05 million, effectively restoring and even exceeding the borrower's original purchasing power.

Finally, the loan professional selects a lender with more flexible guidelines, allowing for higher DTIs and better alignment with the borrower's profile. This ensures that the loan is structured for approval despite the challenging market conditions.

This example demonstrates how advanced structuring can mitigate the impact of rising interest rates. By adjusting variables such as income, debt, and down payment, and by selecting the right lender, the borrower is able to achieve their goals even in a less favorable market.

As you apply these strategies, you will develop the ability to adapt to changing conditions and continue delivering strong results regardless of the market environment.

Chapter 15

The Ultimate Framework—From First Contact to Closing and Beyond

At the final stage of advanced bank statement mortgage loan mastery, everything converges into one unified outcome: a complete, end-to-end framework that takes a borrower from initial contact to closing—and beyond—while maximizing efficiency, consistency, and results. This chapter is about execution at the highest level. It is not about isolated strategies, but about how every piece fits together into a seamless system that produces predictable success.

The ultimate framework begins with the first interaction. Whether the borrower comes from an ad, referral, or organic outreach, the initial conversation sets the tone. Advanced professionals use this moment to quickly identify the borrower's profile, understand their goals, and determine whether a bank statement loan is the right fit. This is not a full analysis, but a high-level filter that allows you to prioritize strong opportunities while setting expectations early.

The next step is structured intake. This involves gathering all relevant information, including bank statements, credit details, debts, reserves, and property goals. At this stage, organization is critical. A consistent intake process ensures that no key information is missed and allows you to move efficiently into analysis. Advanced professionals often use standardized forms or checklists to streamline this process.

Once the data is collected, the process moves into deep analysis and income engineering. This is where your expertise comes into play. You evaluate deposits, remove non-recurring items, apply appropriate expense ratios, and determine the borrower's true qualifying income. At the same time, you assess credit, debt-to-income ratio, loan-to-value, and reserves to understand the overall risk profile.

After analysis, the next step is strategic structuring. This is where you design the loan. You determine the optimal loan amount, select the best time frame for bank statements, decide whether to use personal or business accounts, and identify any compensating factors that can strengthen the file. This step transforms raw data into a structured plan.

Scenario modeling follows. Instead of relying on a single approach, advanced professionals test multiple scenarios. This might include comparing different lenders, adjusting expense ratios, or modifying loan terms. By evaluating these options, you can identify the strategy that provides the best balance of approval likelihood, loan size, and borrower benefit. Lender alignment is the next critical step. Based on your analysis and scenario modeling, you select the lender whose guidelines best match the borrower's profile. This decision is strategic and can significantly impact the outcome of the loan. Advanced professionals maintain a deep understanding of lender overlays and continuously update their knowledge.

Documentation preparation is where the plan becomes actionable. This includes organizing bank statements, preparing income worksheets, creating loan summaries, and ensuring that all documents are complete and consistent. A well-prepared file reduces friction during underwriting and increases the likelihood of a smooth approval.

Submission is not just a technical step—it is a strategic one. Advanced professionals submit files only when all variables are optimized. This includes timing the submission to reflect the strongest possible financial profile and ensuring that all documentation is in place. The goal is to minimize conditions and accelerate the approval process.

During underwriting, communication becomes essential. Responding to conditions quickly, providing clear explanations, and maintaining a collaborative approach with the lender helps keep the process on track. Advanced professionals anticipate potential issues and address them proactively, reducing delays.

Closing is the culmination of the process, but it is not the end. Ensuring that all final documents are accurate, coordinating with all parties involved, and maintaining clear communication helps ensure a successful closing. Attention to detail at this stage is critical to avoid last-minute issues.

Post-closing is where long-term value is created. Following up with the borrower, reviewing the transaction, and identifying future opportunities helps build lasting relationships. Many borrowers will need additional financing in the future, and maintaining this connection creates repeat business.

Another key component of the ultimate framework is continuous improvement. After each deal, advanced professionals review what worked well and what could be improved. This feedback loop allows you to refine your process and increase efficiency over time.

Automation and technology can support this framework by reducing manual tasks and improving consistency. Tools such as CRM systems, document management platforms, and income calculation templates can streamline operations and allow you to focus on high-value activities.

Team integration is also important for scaling this framework. As your volume increases, delegating specific tasks to team members allows you to maintain quality while handling more deals. Clear roles and responsibilities ensure that each part of the process is executed effectively.

Another advanced concept is client experience. Beyond closing the loan, providing a smooth, transparent, and supportive experience creates trust and loyalty. This leads to referrals and repeat business, which are essential for long-term success.

Risk management remains a constant throughout the framework. At every stage, you evaluate and mitigate risk, ensuring that the loan meets guidelines and that the borrower is positioned for success. This protects both the borrower and your business.

Consistency is what turns this framework into a powerful system. By following the same structured approach for each loan, you create predictable outcomes and reduce variability. This consistency allows you to handle complex deals with confidence.

Ultimately, this framework represents the integration of all the skills and strategies you have developed throughout this series. It is a complete system that allows you to consistently structure, approve, and close high-level bank statement mortgage loans.

This is the pinnacle of mastery—not just understanding individual concepts, but executing them seamlessly as part of a cohesive process. By applying this framework, you position yourself as a top-level professional capable of delivering exceptional results.

Real-Life Math Example: Executing the Full Framework from Start to Finish

Consider a self-employed borrower who owns a consulting business and is seeking to purchase a primary residence. The borrower provides 12 months of bank statements showing total deposits of $420,000, averaging $35,000 per month.

During the intake and analysis phase, it is identified that $40,000 of the deposits are non-recurring transfers and should be excluded. This reduces the qualifying deposits to $380,000, resulting in an average monthly deposit of approximately $31,667.

In the income engineering phase, a standard expense ratio of 50% would result in a qualifying income of approximately $15,833 per month. However, the borrower provides a CPA-prepared profit and loss statement showing actual expenses of 35%. Applying this lower expense ratio increases the qualifying income to approximately $20,583 per month.

Next, the risk assessment reveals that the borrower has a credit score of 700, existing debts of $2,500 per month, and $120,000 in reserves. Using a maximum DTI of 50%, the borrower can allocate up to $10,292 toward housing expenses. After subtracting existing debts, the borrower has approximately $7,792 available for a mortgage payment.

At an interest rate of 7%, this supports a loan amount of approximately $1.2 million. However, scenario modeling reveals that by increasing the down payment slightly, the borrower can reduce the loan-to-value ratio and improve pricing.

The lender selection process identifies a lender that allows a 35% expense ratio and offers competitive terms for borrowers with strong credit and reserves. This alignment ensures that the borrower's income is fully optimized.

During documentation preparation, the loan professional creates a detailed income worksheet, organizes all bank statements, and prepares a loan summary that explains the borrower's business and income calculation. This ensures that the file is clear and easy to review.

The loan is submitted at a time when the borrower's financial profile is strong and all variables are optimized. During underwriting, conditions are minimal due to the thorough preparation and clear documentation. At closing, the borrower successfully purchases the property and is positioned for future opportunities. The loan professional follows up after closing, identifying potential refinancing or investment opportunities based on the borrower's goals.

Now consider the alternative scenario where this framework is not applied. Using a standard 50% expense ratio and minimal structuring, the borrower's qualifying income would be significantly lower, resulting in a reduced loan amount or potential denial.

By following the full framework, the loan professional is able to maximize the borrower's income, select the right lender, and present a strong, approvable file. This demonstrates the power of a structured, end-to-end approach.

As you apply this framework consistently, you will develop the ability to handle any scenario with confidence, deliver exceptional results, and build a successful and sustainable mortgage business.

Final Thoughts

Mastery, Momentum, and the Path Forward

As you reach the end of *The Bank Statement Mortgage Loan Mastery Series*, it is important to recognize that this is not an ending—it is a beginning. What you now possess is not just knowledge, but a complete framework, a refined skill set, and a strategic mindset that can be applied to real-world scenarios immediately. You have moved from understanding basic concepts to mastering advanced structuring, from reacting to files to engineering outcomes, and from closing individual deals to building systems that create long-term success.

Throughout this journey, you have learned that bank statement mortgage lending is not simply an alternative loan product—it is a powerful solution for a growing segment of borrowers who do not fit traditional guidelines. Self-employed individuals, business owners, investors, and high-income professionals often face challenges when trying to qualify using tax returns alone. By mastering bank statement loan structuring, you have positioned yourself to serve this underserved market and provide real value where others cannot.

One of the most important takeaways from this series is the concept of control. At the beginner level, it may feel like loan outcomes are determined by rigid guidelines and external factors. However, as you have seen, advanced structuring allows you to influence nearly every aspect of the loan process. From income calculation and expense ratios to lender selection and timing, you have the ability to shape the file in a way that aligns with approval criteria. This level of control is what separates top professionals from the rest.

Another key lesson is the importance of perspective. Every loan file is unique, and there is rarely a single "correct" way to structure it. Instead, there are multiple potential approaches, each with its own advantages and trade-offs. Advanced professionals evaluate these options, compare scenarios, and select the strategy that provides the best outcome. This requires not only technical knowledge but also critical thinking and adaptability.

Consistency is what turns knowledge into mastery. It is not enough to apply these strategies occasionally—you must integrate them into your daily workflow. By following a structured process for each loan, you create predictable outcomes and reduce variability. Over time, this consistency builds confidence, both for you and for your clients, and establishes your reputation as a reliable and effective professional. Another important concept is the power of relationships. Success in this field is not achieved in isolation.

Strong relationships with lenders, underwriters, referral partners, and clients are essential. These relationships provide support, create opportunities, and help you navigate challenges. By maintaining professionalism, communication, and trust, you build a network that enhances your ability to succeed.

The role of education cannot be overstated. Both you and your clients benefit from a deeper understanding of the loan process. By educating borrowers on how their financial behavior impacts their ability to qualify, you empower them to make better decisions. This not only improves the quality of your files but also strengthens your position as a trusted advisor.

Adaptability is another critical factor. The mortgage industry is constantly evolving, with changes in interest rates, lender guidelines, and market conditions. The strategies that work today may need to be adjusted tomorrow. By staying informed and maintaining a flexible mindset, you can continue to provide effective solutions regardless of external changes.

As you move forward, it is important to think beyond individual transactions and focus on long-term impact. Each loan you structure has the potential to change a borrower's financial trajectory. Whether it is helping a business owner purchase their first home, enabling an investor to expand their portfolio, or assisting a borrower in accessing equity, your work has real and lasting consequences. For those looking to scale, the principles in this series provide a foundation for building a high-level business. By creating systems, managing pipelines, and leveraging your expertise, you can increase both volume and efficiency. This allows you to serve more clients while maintaining a high standard of quality.

At the same time, it is important to maintain balance. Growth should be sustainable, and success should not come at the expense of integrity or quality. By adhering to ethical practices and focusing on long-term relationships, you build a business that is not only profitable but also respected.

Another key takeaway is the importance of continuous improvement. No matter how experienced you become, there is always more to learn. Each deal presents an opportunity to refine your approach, identify new strategies, and deepen your understanding. By embracing this mindset, you ensure that your skills remain sharp and your results continue to improve.

Confidence is a natural byproduct of mastery. As you apply these strategies and see the results, you will develop a deeper sense of confidence in your ability to handle complex scenarios. This confidence is not based on guesswork, but on a proven framework and a track record of success.

However, confidence must be balanced with humility. The best professionals remain open to new ideas, seek feedback, and continue to learn from others. This combination of confidence and humility creates a powerful foundation for long-term success.

As you reflect on what you have learned, consider how you will apply it in your own work. Identify the areas where you can improve, the strategies you can implement, and the systems you can build. Take action, even if it is incremental. Progress comes from consistent effort over time.

The future of mortgage lending will continue to evolve, and bank statement loans will play an increasingly important role in serving non-traditional borrowers. By mastering these strategies now, you position yourself at the forefront of this shift, ready to take advantage of new opportunities as they arise.

Your journey does not end here. In many ways, it is just beginning. The knowledge and skills you have developed are tools that you can use to create opportunities, solve problems, and build a successful and fulfilling career. The more you apply them, the more powerful they become.

Remember that mastery is not a destination—it is a process. It is the result of continuous learning, consistent application, and a commitment to excellence. By staying focused, adaptable, and driven, you can achieve results that go beyond what you initially thought possible.

In closing, this series has provided you with a comprehensive roadmap for navigating the world of bank statement mortgage lending at the highest level. You now have the ability to analyze, structure, and close complex loans with confidence and precision. More importantly, you have the mindset and framework needed to continue growing and evolving in this field.

The opportunity is in front of you. The tools are in your hands. The next step is yours to take.

How to Get a Personalized Bank Statement Mortgage Review

If you found this book helpful, you may want to see how these strategies apply to your specific financial situation.

Bank statement mortgage lending is highly customized—your deposits, income patterns, expense ratios, credit profile, property type, and long-term goals all play a role in determining what you qualify for and how your loan should be structured.

Every borrower's situation is different. The way your income flows through your accounts, how your business operates, your credit history, the property you are purchasing or refinancing, and current lender guidelines all impact your options. The strategies and examples in this book are designed to teach you how bank statement mortgage loans work—but your actual qualifying income, loan amount, and loan structure can only be determined by analyzing your real financial profile.

If you would like a no-obligation Bank Statement Mortgage review, you can request one here:

Email: info@FinibiMortgage.com

A licensed mortgage broker will review your bank statements, income structure, credit profile, and goals, and explain what bank statement mortgage options may be available to you—including:

• 12-month and 24-month bank statement programs• Personal vs business bank statement qualification• Primary residence and investment property financing• Cash-out refinance and equity access strategies• Advanced structuring to maximize qualifying income

No cost. No pressure. No obligation.

Sincerely,

Joseph G. Correa

Finibi Mortgage Inc.

Licensed Mortgage Broker

About the Author

Joseph G. Correa is a licensed mortgage broker and the founder of Finibi Mortgage, a Florida-based brokerage specializing in bank statement mortgage loans, non-QM lending, and strategic real estate financing solutions for self-employed borrowers, entrepreneurs, and investors.

With more than two decades of experience in mortgage lending, underwriting, and deal structuring, Joseph has helped thousands of clients qualify for real estate using alternative income documentation, unlocking opportunities that traditional lending often restricts.

Unlike traditional loan officers who rely strictly on tax returns and W-2 income, Joseph's approach focuses on real cash flow, income structuring, and financial strategy. He believes that borrowers should not be limited by how income is reported on paper, but instead empowered by how income is actually earned and managed.

Joseph is widely recognized for his expertise in:

• Bank statement mortgage loans• Self-employed borrower financing• Non-QM and alternative income lending• Investment property and portfolio financing• Cash-out refinance and equity strategies• Advanced mortgage loan structuring

Through his education platform, Finibi Academy, Joseph has trained tens of thousands of students worldwide in mortgage strategy, real estate investing, credit optimization, and financial independence.

He created the **Bank Statement Mortgage Loan Mastery Series** to provide a clear, step-by-step roadmap for borrowers and professionals who want to qualify for real estate without relying on traditional income documentation.

His mission is simple: To help people use their real income—not just their tax returns—to qualify, invest, and build long-term wealth.

When he is not structuring loans or writing, Joseph works with clients across the United States to design customized mortgage strategies that align with their financial goals, income structure, and long-term investment plans.

The Bank Statement Mortgage Loan Mastery Series Roadmap

The Complete Guide to Qualifying for Real Estate Using Bank Statements Instead of Tax Returns

The purpose of the **Bank Statement Mortgage Loan Mastery Series** is to give borrowers, investors, and mortgage professionals the exact strategies used by lenders and underwriters—translated into simple, practical steps you can apply in real life.

This series takes you from beginner to advanced mastery of how to qualify, structure, and scale real estate financing using bank statements instead of traditional income.

Each book builds on the last. You are not just learning how to get approved—you are learning how to control your approvals.

Book 1 — Bank Statement Mortgage Loan Fundamentals

Learn how bank statement loans work, how income is calculated, and why tax returns are no longer required for many borrowers.

Book 2 — Personal Bank Statement Mortgage Loans

Learn how to qualify using personal accounts, structure

deposits, and maximize usable income.

Book 3 — Business Bank Statement Mortgage Loans

Understand how lenders analyze business revenue, apply expense ratios, and use P&Ls.

Book 4 — Bank Statement Loans for Self-Employed Borrowers

Master how entrepreneurs qualify and structure income for approval.

Book 5 — Bank Statement Loans for Primary Residences

Learn how to buy or refinance your home using bank statement income.

Book 6 — Bank Statement Loans for Investment Properties

Discover how to scale rental portfolios using bank statement + DSCR strategies.

Book 7 — Jumbo Bank Statement Mortgage Loans

Learn how to finance high-value properties with advanced requirements and structuring.

Book 8 — Bank Statement Loan Refinancing & Cash-Out Strategies

Unlock equity, reduce payments, and reinvest capital using bank statement refinancing.

Book 9 — Bank Statement Loans with Credit Challenges

Learn how to qualify even with lower credit using compensating factors and strategy.

Book 10 — Advanced Bank Statement Mortgage Loan Structuring

Engineer approvals using deposits, expense ratios, and lender guidelines.

This series is designed to move you from understanding → execution → mastery.

By the end, you will not just know how to qualify—you will know how to structure deals like a professional.

Educational & Financial Disclaimer

The **Bank Statement Mortgage Loan Mastery Series** is intended for educational and informational purposes only.

This content is designed to help readers understand bank statement mortgage lending, real estate financing strategies, and income structuring concepts. It is not financial, legal, tax, or investment advice.

Joseph G. Correa and Live Stronger Faster are not acting as your personal financial advisor, attorney, accountant, or mortgage professional through this publication.

Mortgage guidelines, underwriting standards, interest rates, and loan programs vary by lender and may change at any time without notice.

All examples in this series are for illustration purposes only and do not guarantee approval or results.

Always consult with licensed professionals before making financial decisions.

Risk Disclosure

Bank statement mortgage lending and real estate investing involve risk.

Income fluctuations, interest rate changes, market conditions, and lender guidelines can all impact loan approval and financial outcomes.

Borrowing against real estate or using leverage increases both potential returns and risks.

Failure to repay a loan may result in foreclosure and loss of property.

Cash flow, rental income, and appreciation are not guaranteed.

All strategies in this series are educational and must be evaluated based on your individual financial situation.

You are solely responsible for your financial decisions.